THE NEW ILLUSTRATED GUIDE TO THE

MODERN
US ARMY

SMITHMARK

THE NEW ILLUSTRATED GUIDE TO THE

MODERN
US ARMY

TIM RIPLEY

A Salamander Book

©Salamander Books Ltd. 1992
129-137 York Way, London N7 9LG,
United Kingdom.

ISBN 0-8317-5051-0

This edition published in 1992 by
SMITHMARK Publishers, Inc., 112
Madison Avenue, New York, NY 10016.

SMITHMARK Books are available for
bulk purchase for sales promotion and
premium use. For details write or
telephone the Manager of Special
Sales, SMITHMARK Publishers, Inc.,
112 Madison Avenue, New York, NY
10016. (212) 532-6660.

All correspondence concerning the
content of this volume should be
addressed to Salamander Books Ltd.

This book may not be sold outside the
United States of America or Canada.

Contents

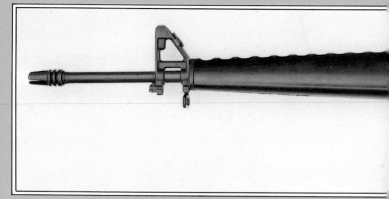

Credits

Author: Tim Ripley is a former research fellow at the University of Oxford. He now makes his living as a full-time author on modern military affairs, contributing to specialist journals.

The author would like to thank Eric C. Ludvigsen, of the Association of the US Army, and Major Peter Keating, of US Army Public Affairs, Pentagon, for their invaluable assistance in the preparation of this title.

Editor: Bob Munro

Designers: Phil Gorton and Bob Munro

Filmset by The Old Mill and Modern Text Typesetting Ltd

Color reproduction by Scantrans Pte.

Printed in Hong Kong

Introduction

As the United States Army entered the 1990s, it had never been so well equipped and trained. During the Gulf War it performed with great skill and professionalism, demonstrating that the ghosts of its disastrous Vietnam involvement were at last fully exorcised.

With the Gulf victory under its belt and the Cold War in Europe all but over, the US Army now faces an equally challenging task — how to live within a shrinking defense budget while retaining its combat power.

The demise of the Soviet threat in Europe has led the US Army to broaden its horizons and concentrate on security problems in other parts of the world. Forward defense of allies by the large-scale deployment of troops overseas is no longer acceptable in the new strategic and financial environment.

US military planners now work on the basis of a forward "presence" to be reinforced in a crisis by rapidly deployed forces from the continental United States. "Reconstitution" of combat forces with mobilised reservists is also a vital element of war plans because of the reductions in active duty soldiers. From its high-point strength in the 1980s of 780,000 active duty soldiers, the US Army plans for a total strength of around 500,000 soldiers in the middle of the 1990s.

High-tech weapons, such as the Patriot missile, M1A1 Abrams tank and AH-64A Apache attack helicopter, may have captured the headlines during the Gulf War but the US Army recognises that its highly trained soldiers were just as important a factor in the American victory as high-technology. Therefore, in the "slimmed down" army of the 1990s, realistic training plays an increasingly important part in ensuring that the US Army is ready to answer any calls to duty quickly and effectively, wherever they come from.

Airland Battle 2000

When US armored and airmobile units blasted their way into southern Iraq during the final days of Operation *Desert Storm* they were putting into practise the US Army's AirLand Battle 2000 fighting doctrine.

America's defeat in Vietnam had traumatised the US Army and led it to look again at its war-fighting doctrine. US military chiefs blamed their defeat in South-East Asia on faulty strategy which locked US forces into a futile war of attrition in the jungles of South Vietnam and prevented them delivering a decisive blow against Communist bases in Laos, Cambodia and North Vietnam. During the 1970s US Army commanders were equally dissastisfied with NATO's linear forward defense strategy in Europe because it lacked any flexibility and looked increasingly like a modern-day version of the "Maginot Line".

These two trends came together in AirLand Battle 2000. It brought back the concept of maneuver as being the decisive factor in warfare and called for military forces to be used aggressively to take the war to the enemy's heartland. The doctrine was formulated in the late-1970s and set out first in the 1982 Field Manual FM 100-5. It calls for air and ground

Above: The ideal military action has a clearly demonstrable aim and is quickly accomplished with minimal casualties. These US Army men in Grenada fulfilled all of these requirements in 1983 as part of Operation *Just Cause*. More recently, and on a greater scale, Operation *Desert Storm* tested the US Army's fighting prowess and combat philosophy in the 100-hour ground war.

forces to be combined to achieve the decisive defeat of the enemy's armed forces. US forces are trained and equipped to destroy the enemy's main forces by surrounding them with armoured thrusts, helicopter assaults into his rear area, and deep air, rocket and artillery strikes against the enemy's command and logistic system. All these operations are to be carried out simultaneously and at a rapid tempo. They must be supported by deception measures and psychological warfare to complete the paralysis of the enemy's command system.

This intense form of warfare certainly had the desired effect on the Iraqi Army, and only four days into the coalition's ground offensive 42 Iraqi divisions were either in full retreat or had been destroyed on the battlefield. Iraq's army could not cope with the rapid pace of the US offensive and was unable to respond.

The first version of FM 100-5 and subsequent 1986 update were focused heavily on high-intensity warfare against Soviet armored forces in the context of NATO's central front. A new version — AirLand Battle Future — looks at applying AirLand Battle 2000's concepts to conflicts in other parts of the world and against a diverse range of opponents.

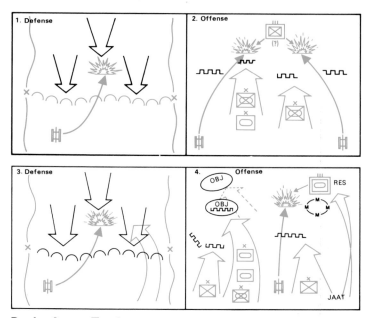

Basic Army Tactics

1—2: *Delay of forces to prevent reinforcement*
At the heart of AirLand Battle 2000 is the concept of striking deep into the enemy's territory to destroy his forces, even during defensive operations. In defense (1) air, artillery and armored forces are used first to directly block enemy thrusts and then strike deep (2) behind his lines to delay or prevent follow-on forces arriving in the battle area. US Army and Marine Corps operations followed this concept in the run-up to the Gulf War ground offensive.

3—4: *Delay in enemy forces to allow maneuver completion*
This concept would have been of critical importance in the event of a Soviet-NATO conflict in Europe. Air power and screening Armored Cavalry forces are used to block the movement of enemy second echelon armored units. This is to prevent interference with friendly forces while they destroy the enemy's first echelon units.

5—6: *Decisive deep attack*
Put into practice in dramatic form during the ground phase of Operation *Desert Storm*. Air, artillery and armored forces drive deep (6) into the enemy's rear area and then destroy key enemy units in detail. Air power and Multiple Launch Rocket Systems (MLRS) play a vital role, striking ahead of the ground units to destroy possible centers of resistance and prevent enemy forces maneuvering to launch counter-attacks. Large forces are also deployed to fix the enemy's first echelon forces (5); to deceive them about the real objectives of US offensive operations and to prevent forces being pulled back in order to engage US forces carrying out the deep strikes. During Operation *Desert Storm*, US Marine Corps and Arab forces fulfilled this fixing role by advancing directly into Kuwait City from the south, while the US VII and XVIII Corps carried out their wide outflanking attack through southern Iraq. Good reconnaissance, electronic

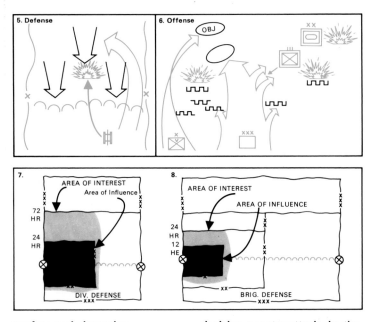

5. Defense

6. Offense

7.
AREA OF INTEREST
Area of Influence
72 HR
24 HR
DIV. DEFENSE

8.
AREA OF INTEREST
AREA OF INFLUENCE
24 HR
12 HE
BRIG. DEFENSE

warfare and deception measures are essential if the enemy's main forces are to be located and US moves shielded from the enemy. By blinding enemy surveillance systems US commanders hope to compound the paralysis of the enemy's command and control system caused by armoured units penetrating deep behind enemy lines.

7: *Organisation of the defense* Defense is considered a temporary phase of war under AirLand Battle 2000. Its only purpose is to buy time for US forces to prepare and mount a decisive counter-attack. In the NATO central front context (7) the balance of forces meant US commanders would have initially had to allow the Soviets to take the initiative in the early phases of any conflict, which would have meant allowing Soviet tank forces to punch through the US covering force screen and into the main defensive position. Reserves had to be held back to counter-attack Soviet penetrations before US forces could strike deep and engage Soviet second and third echelon follow-on forces.

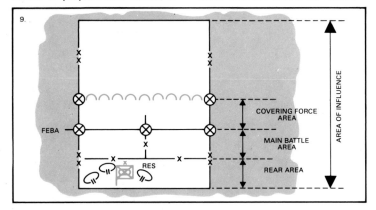

9.
COVERING FORCE AREA
FEBA
MAIN BATTLE AREA
RES
REAR AREA
AREA OF INFLUENCE

Strategy for the 1990s

"Thinking hard about it. I'm running out of demons, I'm running out of villains. I'm down to Fidel Castro and Kim Il Sung" said General Colin Powell, chairman of the Joint Chiefs of Staff in April 1991.

While General Powell may consider the Soviet threat in Europe to be dramatically reduced by *glasnost* and Saddam Hussein has been put in his place by Operation *Desert Storm*, the US Army is now preparing for a new threat — the unknown.

During the 1970s and 1980s the US Army was trained and equipped almost exclusively for war in Central Europe or the Korean peninsula against heavily armored Soviet-style units. Operation *Just Cause* in Panama and Operations *Desert Shield/Desert Storm* showed that the US Army now has to respond rapidly to threats from unexpected directions against many different types of opponent.

A growing range of scenarios for conflict are now receiving the US Army's full attention. The most likely type is classed "peacetime engagement", such as counter-insurgency or anti-drugs operations in support of friendly powers. 'Lesser regional contingencies', such as Operation *Just Cause*, are the next most likely type of operation and would involve small active duty forces. Major regional contingencies in Korea or the Middle East are respectively considered to have a low-to-medium and medium-to-high probability of occurence and would necessitate a major mobilisation of reserves. Global war with the Soviet Union which escalates from a Euro-

Right: The essential raw material of any army is its soldiers. After Vietnam, there was some doubt about the quality and motivation of US soldiers, but their pride and self-confidence has been fully restored after the Gulf War.

pean war is considered very unlikely indeed.

Overwhelming Force

During the 1980s US military chiefs were often criticised by their political masters for being over cautious about involving US military forces in the pursuit of foreign policy objectives. Fear of getting stuck in Vietnam-style wars with no clear objectives or allies was common among military men, who would have had to send the men to do the dying. The bloody fiasco in the Lebanon during the mid-1980s reinforced the views of officers, such as General Powell, who believed that US forces should only be committed to operations that had clear and achievable objectives. Once committed, US forces should be employed in overwhelming numbers with the aim of achieving total victory with minimum loss of life to US troops actively involved.

The doctrine of "overwhelming force" was demonstrated graphically during the intervention in Panama, code-named Operation *Just Cause*, when 22,500 troops supported by hundreds of aircraft and helicopters were sent into action against the drug-dealing General Noriega's ill-equipped "Dignity" Battalions. There was never any doubt about the result, only how long it would take to achieve it.

Right: A US Army soldier takes aim with a Stinger missile unit. The gun versus missile argument has still not been resolved in the area of air defense systems.

Below: A Special Forces combat engineer about to blow a bridge. After a period of neglect, the Special Forces are now in great demand once again.

Low-intensity Operations

Threats to US security are increasingly seen as coming not just from the conventional armies of hostile countries but from non-state groups, such as international drug dealers or terrorist organizations.

During the 1980s the US Army's Special Operations Forces (SOF) were re-organized and equipped to enable them to deal with these new threats. The US Army's Special Forces (*The Green Berets*), *Delta Force* anti-terrorist unit and 160th Special Operations Aviation Group ("*The Night Stalkers*") were placed under the command of the new-tri-service Special Operations Command in a bid to reduce inter-service rivalry and speed up response times to terrorist attacks.

On top of their anti-terrorist duties, the SOF were given the task of taking President George Bush's war on drugs into the heart of the international narcotics network. *Green Beret* teams have been deployed to help Central and South American countries develop their law enforcement capabilities in the face of well-armed and ruthless drugs cartels. In some cases SOFs have participated in raids on the drug barons' heavily defended headquarters.

US Army chiefs have stated that small, mobile and highly trained light forces will be of increasing importance in a world where low-level regional conflicts are likely to be the most prevalent form of warfare. Rapid intervention forces, such as the XVIII Airborne Corps and the 82nd Airborne Division have a secure place in the slimmed down US Army of the 1990s.

The Corps

A US Army corps is an all arms formation, made up of 2-5 combat divisions, and specialist support units such as artillery and combat aviation brigades. A corps usually totals some 100,000 soldiers.

The composition of a corps can vary considerably and is tailored to meet the objectives

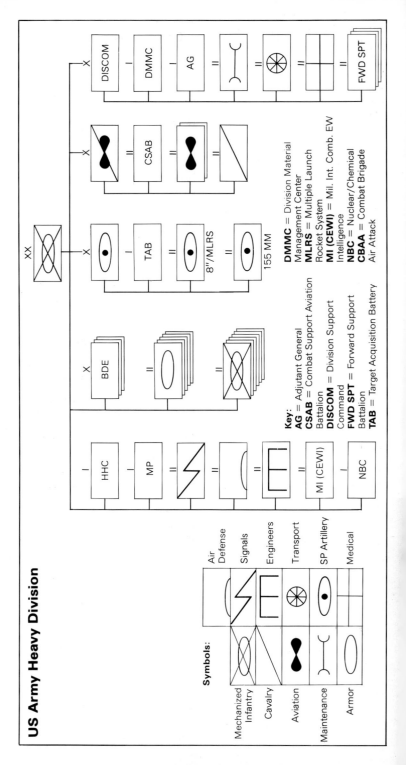

US Army Heavy Division

Symbols:

Mechanized Infantry		Air Defense	
Cavalry		Signals	
Aviation		Engineers	
Maintenance		Transport	
Armor		SP Artillery	
		Medical	

Key:
AG = Adjutant General
CSAB = Combat Support Aviation Battalion
DISCOM = Division Support Command
FWD SPT = Forward Support Battalion
TAB = Target Acquisition Battery

DMMC = Division Material Management Center
MLRS = Multiple Launch Rocket System
MI (CEWI) = Mil. Int. Comb. EW Intelligence
NBC = Nuclear/Chemical
CBAA = Combat Brigade Air Attack

set out by the theater commander. For example, the US VII Corps, which had the task of taking on the Iraqi Republican Guard during Operation *Desert Storm*, boasted three US armoured divisions (1st, 3rd and 1st Cavalry), 1st US Infantry Division (Mechanised) and 1st British Armoured Division. Supporting units included four artillery brigades and a combat aviation brigade.

The US XVIII Airborne Corps, which was tasked by General "Stormin" Norman Schwarzkopf with securing the flank of VII Corps, had the 24th Infantry Division (Mechanised), 101st Airborne Division (Air Assault) and 82nd Airborne Division. The French 6th Light Armoured Division, four US artillery and two aviation brigades were in support.

Corps commanders are provided with extensive communications, electronic warfare and logistic capabilities to enable them to use their subordinate units in the violent and fast moving manner envisaged in the AirLand Battle 2000 doctrine.

The Division

Under the *"Army of Excellence"* programme, US Army divisions are divided into two main

Current Division Forces 1992		
	Active Duty Div (Bdes)	Reserve Component Div (Bdes)
Armor	4 (11) + 2 res bde	2 (6)
Mech Inf	6 (15) + 3 res bde	1 (3)
Motor Inf	1 (2) + 1 res bde	
Air Assault	1 (3)	
Airborne	1 (3)	
Infantry	1 (3)	5 (15)
Lt Infantry	4 (9) + 1 (3)	
Seperate Bdes		
Armor	2	4
Mech Inf	1	2
Inf	2	10
Avn Bde	9	
Armd Car	3	2

types, heavy and light. The former includes armored or cavalry and mechanised infantry divisions. Airborne, air assault, light infantry and mountain divisions are classed as light fighting units.

Heavy divisions are intended to take on opponents who are equipped with strong armored forces and are composed of a mix of 10 armored or mechanised infantry battalions, supported by self-

Below: American soldiers must be prepared to fight anywhere in the world, from Arctic to desert.

propelled artillery and MLRS. Light divisions, which are tailored for combat in difficult terrain or where rapid strategic mobility is required, have nine battalions of infantry and three or four battalions of towed artillery.

Each division is provided with four subordinate brigade headquarters which command combined arms groupings, of up to three to five battalions. One of the brigade headquarters belongs to the division's organic combat aviation brigade and allows the divisional commander to rapidly move firepower and troops around the battlefield.

A mechanised division musters some 16,600 troops, an armoured division 16,300, an air assault division 15,370 and an airborne division 12,790.

Brigades and battalions are termed "maneuver units" and are the division's main combat elements. They are expected to be able to operate either as part of the division's integrated plan or as independent formations if deemed necessary.

Tank Battalion

The cutting edge of the US armored and mechanised units are tank battalions equipped with the M1 or M1A1 Abrams tank. Each unit is equipped with the M1 or M1A1 Abrams tank. A headquarters company contains a cavalry (reconnaissance) and mortar platoon.

During operations it is standard procedure for tank battalions to have their companies split up and attached to task forces formed with mechanised infantry companies and artillery batteries.

In the active duty units the Abrams tank is now the standard main battle tank and the

Below: Post-storage proof firing of TOW missiles by soldiers of 1st Bn, 61st Infantry, at Fort Polk, LA. TOW is one of the best anti-tank guided weapons (ATGWs) in the world.

Above: A TOW missile is launched from an M2 Bradley IFV; one of the vehicles the US Army relies on when it comes to combat.

combat-proven M1A1 is being upgraded to ensure it retains its edge over the Soviet-made tanks until well into the next century.

An increasing number of Army Reserve and National Guard units are starting to receive the M1 in place of their ageing M60s. Those units that still have the M60 are organized into battalions of three companies, each with 17 tanks.

Mechanised Infantry Battalion

A key component in the AirLand Battle 2000 concept is the mechanised infantry. They follow behind the armor to secure ground captured from the enemy or occupy positions for defensive operations.

Active duty and top National Guard "mech inf" battalions field four companies, each with 13 M2 Bradley infantry fighting vehicles. An anti-armor company is attached and fields 12 M901 Improved TOW vehicles. Less-favored National Guard units still have the old M113 armored personnel carrier. These battalions have three companies each with 14 M113s.

The Bradley is more than just a "battlefield taxi", having an impressive weapons fit to allow its embarked infantry squad to fight from their vehicle. Against light or disrupted defenses this capability can reduce infantry casualties to an absolute minimum.

Aviation Brigade

Ever since the Vietnam War the US Army has invested heavily in rotary wing hardware to give

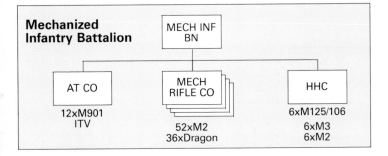

its units mobility, flexibility and airborne firepower. In the Air-Land Battle 2000 concept, helicopters are integrated at divisional level into all types of army formations.

Each division has an aviation brigade, sometimes called a cavalry or combat aviation brigade, which has 18 AH-64A Apache attack helicopters, 25 OH-58 Kiowa scout helicopters and 15 UH-60 Blackhawk transport helicopters. Corps-level units, designated as combat aviation brigades, field 36 Apaches, 26 Kiowas and 15 Blackhawks.

With the night-capable Apache now deployed in most active duty divisions, the aviation brigade is becoming the principal offensive weapon system available to US commanders. During Operation *Desert Storm*, units of VII Corps fielded Apaches ahead of their tanks to blast away with Hellfire missiles any Iraqi troops that attempted to organize coherent defensive positions.

The US Army has long recognised that their aviation brigades are weakened by the lack of fully night-capable and armored scout helicopters. On many occasions during Operation *Desert Storm* Apaches had to be sent on reconnaissance missions because the tactical situation was too dangerous to risk the unarmored OH-58C/Ds. To fill this gap in its inventory the US Army is to field the Boeing/Sikorsky RAH-66

Commanche Scout 5 attack helicopter by the year 2000.

Divisional Artillery
The introduction of the MLRS system into divisional artillery units has transformed the deep strike capabilities of US Army divisions. Rocket-assisted projectiles (RAP) have also improved the range of conventional tube artillery.

Currently, divisional artillery in armored and mechanised divisions comprise three field artillery battalions (each with three batteries of eight M109 self-propelled howitzers), a battery of nine MLRS and a target acquisition battery. M109 batteries are often assigned to support armored or mechanised infantry task forces. Light infantry and National Guard units use a variety of systems, including towed 105mm and 155mm guns and the old M110 self-propelled 8in howitzer.

Computerised fire-control and ammunition management systems have been introduced to speed up the ability of US commanders to deliver fire and to reduce wastage of ammunition. The success of the Copperhead "smart" artillery round in the Gulf war has stimulated interest in such weapons and the US Army is looking to develop the "fire and forget" Sense and Destroy Armor (SADARM) round. With such rounds it is hoped to transform artillery from area weapons into precision tank killers.

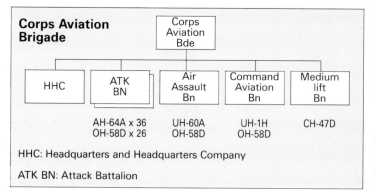

Corps Aviation Brigade		Corps Aviation Bde		
HHC	ATK BN	Air Assault Bn	Command Aviation Bn	Medium lift Bn
	AH-64A x 36 OH-58D x 26	UH-60A OH-58D	UH-1H OH-58D	CH-47D

HHC: Headquarters and Headquarters Company

ATK BN: Attack Battalion

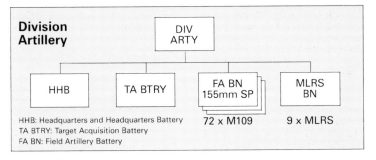

Division Artillery

```
                    ┌─────────┐
                    │   DIV   │
                    │  ARTY   │
                    └────┬────┘
        ┌────────────┬───┴────────────┬────────────┐
   ┌────┴────┐  ┌────┴────┐     ┌─────┴─────┐  ┌────┴────┐
   │   HHB   │  │ TA BTRY │     │  FA BN    │  │  MLRS   │
   │         │  │         │     │ 155mm SP  │  │   BN    │
   └─────────┘  └─────────┘     └───────────┘  └─────────┘
```

HHB: Headquarters and Headquarters Battery
TA BTRY: Target Acquisition Battery
FA BN: Field Artillery Battery

72 x M109   9 x MLRS

Budget Cuts

In line with other western countries the United States has instigated a program of large-scale defense cuts in response to the collapse of the Warsaw Pact. The President and congressional leaders set a target of a 25 per cent overall cut in defense spending in the first half of the 1990s.

For the US Army this means the loss of over 200,000 active duty soldiers, the disbandment of eight divisions and the closure of many foreign and Stateside bases. Outline plans envisage a 20-division army with an active duty force built around four corps and 12 divisions. Most of the cuts fall on units based in Germany or those earmarked to reinforce NATO in time of conflict.

The US Army in Europe is to be cut by at least half, with forces in Germany eventually consisting of two divisions in

Below: The Multiple Launch Rocket System (MLRS) is an awesome addition to the US Army's firepower arsenal. It fires 12 rockets per launch

a single corps, as opposed to the 1980s force of two corps and four divisions. Single divisions remain in South Korea and Hawaii.

While in the past only a few units such as the 82nd Airborne and 101st Airborne (Air Assault) Divisions were slated for "contingency" operations, in future all US Army units will be prepared to participate in rapid deployment activities rather than just concentrating on a single threat scenario, such as the defense of NATO's central front. The move of VII Corps from Germany to the Gulf during Operation *Desert Storm* is seen as the model for the future operational role of forward-deployed units.

Total Force

With the loss of six active-duty divisions, the US Army is going to increasingly depend on the "weekend warriors" of the Army Reserve and Army National Guard to "reconstitute" large combat forces for major military operations.

The reserve components currently provides 54 per cent of the US Army's combat units (infantry, armor, artillery), 58 per

cent of combat support (signals, military police and engineer, etc) and 70 per cent of service support (quartermaster, transportation and medical, etc).

During Operation *Desert Storm*, 80,000 Guard and reserve soldiers were deployed to the Middle East to provide important logistic and medical support to active-duty units. Two brigades of National Guard artillery went into battle in support of British and American units advancing into southern Iraq. Some 136,000 Guardsmen and 90,000 reserve soldiers, along with two divisions, are planned to be cut, but the large scale cutbacks in active-duty units mean that the reserve component will have an even more crucial role in the US Army during the late-1990s.

Active-duty units are seen as being able to cope with limited contingencies, such as the Panama intervention, but for large operations that require sustained deployments the mobilization of significant numbers of reservists will be essential.

Conclusion

US Army Chief of Staff General Carl Vuono proudly stated in June 1991 that the US Army had won three victories in the past four years — the defeat

Below: The arduous conditions in Iraq and Kuwait tested US Army force mobility to the full.

of Iraq in the Gulf War, the invasion of Panama and the winning of the Cold War in Europe.

Peace, however, brings its own problems and General Vuono has pledged not to repeat the mistakes of the rapid disarmament after World War II. This reduced the effectiveness of the Army to such an extent that it found itself without combat ready forces to

Above: These men of the US Army Reserve are an integral part of mobilization plans.

deploy instantly to turn back the Communist advance into South Korea in 1950. The US Army of the next century will be ready and able to take on all comers, even if it is a much smaller organization than that of the 1980s.

Main Battle Tanks

The outstanding performance of the M1A1 Abrams in the "100 Hour" offensive into southern Iraq during the final phase of the Gulf War confirmed the US's considerable lead in Main Battle Tank technology.

In World War Two the US Army relied on overwhelming numbers of "low-tech" Sherman tanks to defeat the technologically superior German Tiger and Panther tanks. Since

---

Abrams, M1A1 and M1

Type: Main battle tank.
Crew: Four.
Armament: One 120mm M256 smooth-bore gun (M1A1); one 105mm M68 gun (M1); one 7.62mm co-axial machine-gun; one 0.50in machine-gun on commander's cupola; one M240 7.62mm machine-gun on loader's hatch.
Armor: Chobham armor. M1A1 (HE) has depleted uranium armor.
Dimensions: Length (gun forward) 32ft 0½in (9.77m); length (hull) 25ft 11¾in (7.92m); width 11ft 11¾in (3.66m); height 7ft 9½in (2.38m).
Weight: Combat loaded 149,950lb (68,075kg).
Engine: Avco Lycoming AGT-T 1500 HP-C turbine developing 1,500hp.
Performance: Top speed 41.5mph (66.77km/h); range 275 miles (443km); vertical obstacle 4ft 1in (1.24m); trench 9ft (2.73m); gradient 60 per cent
History: First production vehicle completed in 1980.

The M1A1 Abrams tank is the US Army's primary combat weapon for closing with and destroying the enemy. Its 120mm smooth-bore cannon and Thermal Imaging System give it immense hitting power at ranges up to 3,991 yards (3,650m), in all weathers and at night. Chobham and depleted uranium armor ensure unparalleled survivability, even from direct hits.

Development of the Abrams began in 1973 after the collapse of the MBT-70 project. Chrysler won a competition for the Abrams contract against the General Motors Corporation and production of the first version, the M1, began in 1979 at the Detroit Arsenal Tank Plant. Initial vehicles were ▶

1945, the US has been trying to develop a technological lead to overcome the staggering numerical superiority of the Soviet Union's vast tank force.

Until the 1980s that quest was dogged by cost overruns, technological disasters and reliance on *ad hoc* improvements to ageing designs, such as the M48 and M60. With the M1A1, the US Army at last has a winner. When matched face-to-face with the top Soviet tank — the T-72 — the M1A1s of the US Army's VII Corps came away with hardly a scratch on their paintwork. No M1A1s were penetrated by Iraqi tank fire and from early reports it seems that US Army tank crews were in more danger from "friendly fire" from other M1A1s than from the Soviet-equipped Iraqi forces!

Above: The M1 Abrams main battle tank has taken many years to reach combat units but is now in service in very considerable numbers.

Far left: A prototype M1 fires its British-designed 105mm rifled main armament. The later M1A1 sports a 120mm smooth-bore gun.

Left: Churning up the mud as it ploughs onwards on a NATO exercise, this M1 makes a formidable sight to any enemy force ahead.

Above: The M1 has a 27 per cent lower silhouette than the M60A1 but with the same ground clearance of about 19 inches (48cm).

delivered to the US Army the following year and the first units were operational in 1982. General Dynamics Land Systems now produce the Abrams after taking over Chrysler's tank business during 1982.

During its production run a series of upgrades have taken place to improve the Abrams, with five main versions now in US Army service. The basic M1 has the British-designed M68 105mm rifled cannon as its main armament, and is protected by British-designed Chobham armor. Some 2,734 were produced up until 1984. Next off the Detroit assembly line was the IPM1, which was an interim model between the old M1 and the M1A1. The 894 IPM1s built field the improved turret armor of the M1A1 but not its 120mm gun.

In 1985, the M1A1 started to enter service with US Army tank units in Germany. The fitting of the German Rheinmetall 120mm M256 gun had always been considered as a future upgrade, and the Abrams was designed with this in mind. However, problems were still encountered adapting the turret to take the new gun. Other improvements included a pressurized-air Nuclear, Biological and Chemical Warfare protection system, improved armor, better suspension and microclimate cooling system. Current plans call for 4,576 M1A1s to be purchased for the US Army. By 1991, some 3,884 units had been produced.

To provide protection from direct hits by enemy tank guns, the US Army and General Dynamics started a secret program to develop depleted uranium armor for the M1A1. The resulting M1A1 (Heavy Armor) entered production in 1988, and by 1991 1,500 had been delivered to the US Army. ▶

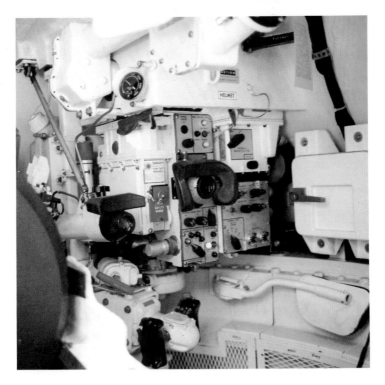

Above: The gunner's position inside the turret of the M1. The ever increasing sophistication of MBTs is leading to spiralling costs.

Below: At the height of the Cold War, an M1 Abrams makes its way through a village street in what was formerly West Germany.

▶ The final version of the Abrams is designated the M1A2 and during 1991 was undergoing full-scale development to improve its survivability, target acquisition, fire control and reliability.

During the 1980s, the US Army followed a policy of delivering its newest tanks to the units facing the greatest threat: those assigned to the US Army in Europe. So a rolling program of re-equipment took place, with Germany-based units receiving the M1, then the IPM1 and, most recently, the M1A1/M1A1(HE). Active duty units based in the continental USA, followed by reserve units with a NATO reinforcement role, would then receive the less modern versions of the Abrams from Germany as the frontline units took delivery of their factory-fresh tanks. It is intended that all active duty units will field the M1A1 by the end of 1992.

When the 24th Infantry Division (Mechanized) and 1st Cavalry Division were deployed to Saudi Arabia in September 1990, they had yet to receive the M1A1, so 750 of the new-model tanks were shipped from POMCUS stores in Germany to re-equip the two divisions in-theatre. All VII Corps divisions already fielded the M1A1 when they were ordered to Saudi Arabia, and the US Army made an effort to send as many M1A1(HA)s as possible to the Middle East By the time the ground offensive began in February 1991, some 27 per cent of the 1,956 Abrams in theatre were M1A1(HE)s, ▶

Right: Equipped with an M68 105mm rifled cannon, this is one of over 3,600 M1/IPM1 Abram's built with this armament.

Below: In addition to its British-designed main cannon, the M1 is protected by British-designed Chobham armor-plating.

and the remainder had an extra armor plate welded onto their turret fronts. The US Army's up-armoring efforts paid off: seven M1A1s received hits from T-72 rounds during the brief ground war, but the Soviet shells just bounced off and caused no damage. The T-72's armor was equally ineffective as the M1A1's 120mm gun easily penetrated even the frontal armor of

Below: An M1A1 Abrams MBT at speed is an awesome sight, as the Iraqi Army found out when faced with scores of these well-armed, well-protected machines bearing down on them during the short ground war within Operation *Desert Storm*.

the Soviet tank. Sand berms also provided little protection from the M829A1 sabot round. US tank crews reported that the M1A1's Thermal Imaging Sight gave them a great advantage over Iraqi tanks because it had a longer range than the Soviet-made systems, and could also see through the smoke from burning oil wells.

As predicted by many pundits, the M1A1's turbine engine proved to be a gas guzzler. US tank units had to refuel their M1A1's every three to five hours to ensure that they always went into combat with full tanks and only a massive logistic effort prevented the advance into Iraq grinding to a halt from lack of fuel.

M60
M60, M60A1, M60A3, M60 AVLB, M728 CEV

Type: Main battle tank.

Crew: 4.

Armament: One 105mm gun; one 7.62mm machine gun co-axial with main armament; one 0.50in anti-aircraft machine gun in commander's cupola.

Armor: 12.7mm-120mm (0.5-4.80in).

Dimensions: Length (gun forward) 30ft 11in (9.436m); length (hull) 22ft 9½in (6.946m); width 11ft 11in (3.631m); height 10ft 8in (3.257m).

Weight: Combat 114,600lb (51,982kg).

Ground pressure: 11.24lb/in² (0.79kg/cm²).

Engine: Continental AVDS-1790-2A 12-cylinder diesel developing 750bhp at 2,400rpm.

Performance: Road speed 30mph (48km/h); range 280 miles (450km); vertical obstacle 3ft (0.914m); trench 8ft 6in (2.49m); gradient 60 per cent.

History: The M60 entered service with the US Army in 1960 and is also used by Austria, Egypt, Ethiopia, Iran, Israel, Italy, Jordan, Morocco, Saudi Arabia, Somalia, South Korea, Tunisia, Turkey, US Marine Corps, Yemen Arab Republic (North). (*Note that the Specifications relate to the M60A3 model*).

For most of the 1970s and into the early-1980s, the M60 was the US Army's standard Main Battle Tank. It was superceded by the M1 series in Germany in the mid-1980s and should be retired from all active duty tank units by the end of 1992. However, the Army National Guard will continue to use the vintage M60 for many years to come. Some 7,000 M60s are still in the US Army's inventory although a major campaign is underway to sell them off to Third World countries.

The M60 was a natural development of the tried and tested M48 tank and it shared many features, including a similar internal layout. The new tank also sported a flat front glacis and a new turret to enable the British designed M68 105mm gun to be used. An up-armored turret was subsequently developed for the M60A1.

No M60 Main Battle Tanks saw service in Vietnam, but the Israelis used them extensively in the 1973 Yom Kippur War and during the 1982 invasion of Lebanon. The M60 saw its first combat use in US hands with the US Marine Corps during the ill-fated intervention in Lebanon in the mid-1980s, and Egyptian and Saudi armored units employed the M60 during the Gulf War. Iranian tank units also used the M60 in their eight-year war with ▶

Below: The Commander and Gunner of an M60 confer over a map during a winter exercise in Germany. The vehicle immediately to the rear is a standard battle tank fitted with a dozer blade.

Above: An M60 moves through a German town. By the mid-1980s, all US Army M60s in German had been replaced by M1 Abrams MBTs.

▶ Iraq during the 1980s.

Around a third of the current US inventory of M60s are M60A1s, which entered production in 1962. During the 1970s the M60A3 replaced it as the US Army's principal tank. The new model featured a TTS thermal imaging sight, main armament stablization, laser range-finder, solid state ballistic computer, thermal gun sleeve, engine smoke generator and RISE engine as standard.

In 1974 252 M60A2s entered service with the US Army in Germany, but there were constant problems with the tanks' 152mm Shillelagh gun/missile system and they were retired in the early-1980s. A more successful modification was the M728 Combat Engineer Vehicle which

Below: The M60A2 had an unusual 152mm gun/missile launcher, but technical problems led to its early withdrawal from service.

Above: An M60 crosses a floating bridge on exercise. Orange markings show that this example is with the "enemy" forces.

is equipped with a dozer blade, 152mm demolition gun and an A-frame for moving obstacles. Mine-clearing rollers can also be fitted.

The M60A1 and M60A3 proved to be very reliable tanks and they were very popular with their crews. The simplicity and ease of maintenance of the tank led many US Army tankmen who converted to the complex new Abrams to long for the "good old" M60. For many years the M60's capabilities *vis-a-vis* Soviet tanks were the subject of much speculation, particularly after the introduction of the T-72. The argument was settled for good when M60A1s from the 1st Marine Division encountered 70 Iraqi T-72s at Kuwait International Airport on 26 February 1991 and destroyed them all, along with 180 T-55s and T-62s for good measure.

Below: A specialized version of the M60 is the M728 Combat Engineer Vehicle, with a dozer blade and 152mm gun.

Armored Personnel Carriers

When the Soviets fielded their BMP infantry fighting vehicle (IFV) in 1967, it revolutionized thinking about providing armored vehicles to transport infantrymen into battle. In response the US Army began developing its own IFV to replace the M113 armored personnel carrier. The M113 performed well

M2/M3

Type: (M2) Infantry Fighting Vehicle; (M3) Cavalry Fighting Vehicle.
Crew: 3 plus 6.
Armament: One 25mm Hughes ''chain-gun'', one 7.62mm machine-gun co-axial with main armament; twin launcher for Hughes TOW ATGW.
Armor: Classified.
Dimensions: Length 21ft 2in (6.45m); width 10ft 6in (3.20m); height 9ft 9in (2.97m).
Weight: 50,000lb (22,680kg).
Ground pressure: 7.7lb/in² (0-54kg/cm²).
Engine: Cummins VTA-903T water-cooled 4-cycle diesel developing 506bhp.
Performance: Road speed 41mph (66km/h); water speed 4.5mph (7.24km/h); range 300 miles (384km); vertical obstacle 3ft (0.91m); trench 8ft 4in (2.54m); gradient 60 per cent.
History: Entered US Army service in 1983.

Below: An M2 Bradley Infantry Fighting Vehicle (IFV) at speed, showing its excellent agility, which equates with that of the larger and heavier M1 Abrams Main Battle Tank.

in the jungles of Vietnam as a "battlefield taxi", but it was not considered up to the job of carrying infantry into the heart of a major tank battle.

During its baptism of fire in the Gulf War, the M2/M3 Bradley Fighting Vehicle System validated the US Army's IFV concept. Bradleys kept up with the Abrams tanks during the "100 Hour" ground offensive into southern Iraq, ensuring that infantry were always on hand to clear Iraqi defensive positions and allowing the advance to maintain its momentum. The Bradley's impressive weapons fit enabled its crews to fight from their vehicles and US mechanized infantry only had to dismount to collect Iraqi prisoners.

Throughout the 1960s the US Army was keen to develop an IFV, but its experimental projects did not result in any satisfactory vehicles being fielded. In 1972 the FMC Corporation, builders of the M113, began work on the XM723, which by 1976 had become the M2/M3 Bradley Fighting Vehicle System (BFVS).

The primary task of the M2 in the eyes of the US Army is to enable infantry to fight from under armor whenever practicable, and to be able both to observe and to use their weapons from inside the vehicle. The M2 will replace some, but not all, of the current M113 APCs, as the latter are more than adequate for many roles on the battlefield. The M2 has three major advances over the existing M113 APC. First, the IFV has greater mobility and better cross-country speed, enabling it to keep up with the M1 MBT when acting as part of the tank/infantry team. Second, it has much greater firepower. Third, it has superior armor protection. The tank provides long-range firepower whilst the IFV provides firepower against softer, close-in targets. The M2's infantry also assist tanks by locating and destroying enemy anti-tank weapons. ▶

Below: An infantry squad "debussing" from its M2. The small size of the crew compartment at the rear of the vehicle has reduced the complement of the dismounting squad to six soldiers.

Above: Kicking up the dust during an exercise at one of the US Army's designated training areas, this M2 IFV sports infra-red laser sensors to record "hits" by "enemy" forces. Visible just below the 7.62mm gun is a quartet of smoke dischargers.

Left: The operational versatility of the M2/M3 is enhanced by its fully amphibious qualities. When in the water, the vehicle is propelled at a modest speed by its tracks. Performance in water is restricted to 4.5mph (7.24km/h).

The hull of the M2 is of all-welded aluminum construction with an applique layer of steel armor welded to the hull front, upper sides and rear for added protection. The hull sides also have a thin layer of steel armor, the space between the aluminum and steel being filled with foam to increase the buoyancy of the vehicle. The armored protection of the IFV is claimed to be effective against Soviet 14.5mm armor-piercing rounds and 155mm air-burst shell splinters.

The driver is seated at the front of the vehicle on the left, with the engine to his right. The two-man turret is in the center of the hull and the personnel ▶

Above: An M2 Bradley IFV on the firing range. Note the prominent box on the near-side of the two-man turret which is a twin TOW anti-tank missile launcher.

Above: An M2 negotiates a cross-country driving course. The M2's main gun is a single Hughes 25mm "chain gun"; to its right is a 7.62mm co-axial machine-gun.

Left: The launch by an M2 of a TOW anti-tank missile is recorded on high-speed film. The armament carried by the M2/M3 greatly enhances the firepower available to US Army infantry battalions.

▶ compartment is at the rear. Personnel entry is effected through a large power-operated ramp in the hull rear. The two-man power-operated turret is fully stabilized and is armed with a 25mm Hughes Chain Gun and a co-axial 7.62mm machine gun. The weapons can be elevated to + 60° and depressed to − 10°, turret traverse being 360°. Mounted on the left side of the turret is a twin launcher for the Hughes TOW ATGW. A total of 900 rounds of 25mm, 2,340 rounds of 7.62mm and seven TOW missiles are carried. The troop compartment is provided with six firing ports (two in each side and two at the rear) for the 5.56mm M231 weapon. The M231 is a specially developed version of the M16, cut-down and sealed in a ball mount. It is somewhat ironic that the outcome of a requirement for the infantry to be able to use their weapons from inside the vehicle should be an additional and specialized rifle. Internal storage allows the M2's infantry squad to be equipped with a Dragon anti-tank missile. A thermal imaging sight is fitted as standard.

The M2's sister vehicle, the M3 Cavalry Fighting Vehicle (CFV), is issued to armored cavalry units for reconnaissance, screening and security work. The CFV lacks the M2's firing ports and only carries two infantrymen in the rear compartment. This allows extra 25mm ammunition and 10 TOW missile reloads to be carried.

Up until 1991 it was planned to purchase some 9,000 M2/M3s, but budget cuts have scaled down the US Army's requirement and now production is to cease in 1995/96, by which time some 6,724 vehicles will be in US Army service. In 1987 M2A1/M3A1s were modified to fire the improved TOW-2 missile. The current production versions, designated the M2A2/M3A2, feature bolt-on reactive armor and a 600hp engine.

Both versions of the Bradley performed well in the Gulf War. Its thermal sight was judged to be more effective than the Iraqi systems and gave cavalry units a big edge during their reconnaissance operations, even in sand storms. For many years the Bradley's transmission has been dogged by problems but none failed during the "100 Hour" offensive. The 25mm cannon was reported to be more effective than crews expected. M2A2/M3A2s were particularly popular with their crews because of their extra power and armor protection.

M113

M113, M113A1, M113A2, M113A3, M106, M132, M163 and variants.

Type: Armored personnel carrier.
Crew: 2 plus 11.
Armament: One Browning 0.5in (12.7mm) machine-gun.
Armor: 0.47-1.58in (12-38mm).
Dimensions: Length 15ft 11in (4.863m); width 8ft 10in (2.686m); height 8ft 2in (2.5m).
Weight: Combat 24,600lb (11,156kg).
Ground Pressure: 7.82lb/in² (0.55kg/cm²).
Engine: General Motors Model 6V53 six-cylinder water-cooled diesel developing 215bhp at 2,800rpm.
Performance: Road speed 42mph (67.6km/h); water speed 3.6mph (5.8km/h); range 300 miles (483km); vertical obstacle 2ft (0.61m); trench 5ft 6in (1.68m); gradient 60 per cent.
History: Entered service with the United States Army in 1960. Also used by 50 other countries.

In the early-1950s the standard United States Army APC was the M75, followed in 1954 by the M59. Neither of these was satisfactory and in 1954 foundations were laid for a new series of vehicles. In 1958 prototypes of the T113 (aluminium hull) and T117 (steel hull) armored personnel carriers were built. A modified version of the T113, the T113E1, was cleared for production in mid-1959 and production commenced at the FMC plant at San Jose, California, in 1960. The vehicle is still in production today and some 70,000 have been built in the USA. It is also built in Italy by Oto Melara, which has produced a further 4,000 for the Italian Army and for export. In 1964 the M113 was replaced in production by the M113A1, identical with the earlier model but for a diesel rather than a petrol engine.
   The M113A1 had a larger radius of action than the earlier vehicle. The M113 had the distinction of being the first armored fighting vehicle of ▶

Below: The squat outline of the M113 is distinctive even amidst the snows of Alaska, as a squad from "A" Company, 1st BG/23rd Infantry, goes through a tactical deployment demonstration in the Fort Richardson training aids area.

Above: More M113 chassis have been built than any other since 1945. Illustrated is the M557 unarmed command post version.

Below: A pair of M113s in convoy pass through a German town during a *Reforger* (REturn of FORces to GERmany) exercise. Although unable to keep pace with the M2/M3 Bradley IFV, the M113 can carry out duties for which the Bradley is unsuitable.

aluminium construction to enter production. The driver is seated at the front of the hull on the left, with the engine to his right. The commander's hatch is in the center of the roof and the personnel compartment is at the rear of the hull. The infantry enter and leave via a large ramp in the hull rear, although there is also a roof hatch over the troop compartment. The basic vehicle is normally armed with a pintle-mounted Browning 0.5in machine-gun, which has 2,000 rounds of ammunition. The M113 is fully amphibious and is propelled in the water by its tracks. Infra-red driving lights are fitted as standard. FMC has developed a wide variety of kits for the basic vehicle including an ambulance kit, NBC kit, heater kit, dozer-blade kit, various shields for machine-guns, and so on.

There are more variants of the M113 family than any other fighting vehicle in service today, and there is room here to mention only some of the more important models. The M577 is the command model, with a much higher roof and no armament. There are two mortar carriers: the M125 with an 81mm mortar, and the M106 with a 107mm mortar. The flame-thrower model is known as the M132A1, and is not used outside ▶

Left: The M901 Improved TOW vehicle (ITV), whose missile components can be removed for ground-launching if tactically necessary.

Below: The M48 Chaparral forward area air-defense system is a variant of the M548, based on the M113 chassis.

Above: One of the myriad derivatives of the basic M113 APC is the M981 Fire Support Team Vehicle (FISTV) for artillery observers.

Right: An M113A3 APC cuts up the dust on a US Army test range. Note the external fuel cells visible at the rear of the hull.

▶ the United States Army. The M806 is the recovery model, and this is provided with a winch in the rear of the vehicle and spades at the rear. The anti-aircraft model is known as the Vulcan Air Defense System or M163; this is armed with a six-barrelled 20mm General Electric cannon. The M548 tracked cargo carrier is based on an M113 chassis, can carry 5 tons (5,080kg) of cargo and is fully amphibious. There are many models of the M548, including the M727, which carries three HAWK surface-to-air-missiles, and the M730, which carries four Chaparral short-range surface-to-air-missiles. Yet another version, the M752, carries the Lance tactical missile system, whilst the M688 carries two spare missiles.

One recent model is the M901 Improved TOW Vehicle (ITV), with a retractable launcher that carries two Hughes TOW ATGWs.

Deliveries of the latest model, the M113A3, began in 1986 and the current US Army contract is scheduled for completion in 1991. It features spall suppression liners, armored external fuel tanks, an upgraded engine, improved transmissions, and mounting points for bolt-on armor. A depot conversion program is underway to upgrade existing M113A2s to the new standard. It is envisaged that the M113A3 will continue to serve for many years in roles for which the Bradley IFV is unsuitable, such as engineer squad carriers, armored ambulance, maintenance support vehicle and command vehicle. The M113 family came in for harsh criticism during Operation *Desert Storm* because the ITV, command post and fire-support versions could not keep up with the Abrams tanks and Bradley IFVs during cross-country operations.

Above: An infantry squad debussing from an M113, virtually the standard APC in Western-oriented armies since the 1960s.

Reconnaissance Vehicles

For financial reasons the US Army gave up fielding purpose-built reconnaissance vehicles in the mid-1970s, when it decided to use a version of the Bradley IFV for scouting work. Since then it has used the M3 CFV, Abrams tanks and helicopters as

M93 Fox

Type: NBC reconnaissance vehicle.
Crew: 4 (3 on systems-improved version).
Armament: Nil.
Dimensions: Length 22.2ft (7.74m); width 9.6ft (2.9m); height 7.5ft (2.3m).
Armor: Effective protection from small arms and artillery fire.
Weight: 16.7 tons (16,968kg).
Engine: Mercedes Benz OM-402V8 Diesel (320hp).
Performance: Top road speed 65mph (165km/h); range 497 miles (800km).

The M93 Fox Nuclear, biological and Chemical Reconnaissance System (NBCRS) is the newest armored vehicle to enter service with the US Army. From the protection of the vehicle, crew members are able to detect, identify and mark areas of NBC contamination, collect soil, water and

main reconnaissance platforms in armored cavalry regiments and divisional cavalry squadrons.

The last purpose-built reconnaissance vehicle to be developed, the M551 Sheridan, was considered one of the US Army's worst tanks ever. Its only saving grace was its airportability, which has allowed it to soldier on with the 82nd Airborne Division.

Saddam Hussein's chemical weapons threat made the US Army realize that it had a yawning gap in its capability to detect chemical contamination. The Germany *Bundeswehr* came to the rescue and gave the US Army and Marine Corps 50 of its Fox specialist reconnaissance vehicles.

---

vegetation samples for later analysis and transmit NBC warning information to higher commanders. The Fox's internal overpressure atmosphere systems protects its crew from chemical threats.

To mark areas of contamination, warning flags can be automatically positioned by the vehicle. A system of scoops and air locks allows the crew to collect samples. There is also a rubber arm glove so crewmen can carry out complicated NBC sampling without leaving the vehicle. The Fox also carries a wide range of NBC sampling and testing kits.

In addition to 40 systems donated by the *Bundeswehr* (10 more went to the US Marine Corps), the US Army plans an initial buy of 54 from Thyssen Henschel. World-wide fielding will follow after a Systems Improvement Phase to be undertaken by General Dynamics Land System in the United States.

Below: One of the 40 Fox NBC reconnaissance vehicles supplied to the US Army by Germany for use during the Gulf War.

M551 Sheridan

Type: Light tank.
Crew: 4.
Armament: One 152mm gun/missile launcher; one 7.62mm machine-gun co-axial with main armament; one 0.5in anti-aircraft machine-gun; four smoke dischargers on each side of turret.
Armor: Classified.
Dimensions: Length 20ft 8in (6.299m); width 9ft 3in (2.819m); height (overall) 9ft 8in (2.946m).
Weight: Combat 34,898lbs (15,830kg).
Ground pressure: 6.96lb/in² (0.49kg/cm²).
Engine: Detroit Diesel 6V53T six-cylinder diesel developing 3000bhp at 2,800rpm.
Performance: Road speed 45mph (70km/h); water speed 3.6mph (5.8km/h); range 373 miles (600km); vertical obstacle 2ft 9in (0.838m); trench 8ft 4in (2.54m); gradient 60 per cent.
History: Entered service with United States Army in 1966 and still in service.

In August 1959 the United States Army established a requirement for a "new armored vehicle with increased capabilities over any other weapon in its own inventory and that of any adversary". The following year the Allison Division of General Motors was awarded a contract to design a vehicle called the Armored Reconnaissance Airborne Assault Vehicle (ARAAV) to meet the requirement. The first prototype, designated XM551, was completed in 1962, and this was followed by a further 11 prototypes. Late in 1965 a production contract was awarded to Allison, and the first production vehicles were completed in 1966, these being known as the M551 or Sheridan. Production was completed in 1970 after a total of 1,700 vehicles had been built.

The·hull of the Sheridan is of all-aluminium construction whilst the turret is of welded steel. The driver is seated at the front of the hull and the other three crew members are in the turret, with the loader on the left and the gunner and commander on the right.

There are no track-return rollers. The most interesting feature of the Sheridan is its armament system. This consists of a 152mm gun/launcher which has an elevation of +19° and a depression of —8°, traverse being 360°. A 7.62mm machine-gun is mounted co-axially with the main armament,

and there is a 0.5in Browning machine-gun on the commander's cupola. The latter cannot be aimed and fired from within the turret, and as a result of combat experience in Vietnam many vehicles have now been fitted with a shield for this weapon. The 152mm gun/launcher, later fitted to the M60A2 and MBT-70 tanks, can fire either a Shillelagh missile or a variety of conventional ammunition including HEAT-T-MP, WP and canister, all of them having a combustible cartridge case. The Shillelagh missile was developed by the United States Army Missile Command and the Philco-Ford Corporation, and has a maximum range of about 3,281 yards (3,000m). The missile is controlled by the gunner, who simply has to keep the cross-hairs of his sight on the target to ensure a hit; however severe problems exist in "capturing" the missile, making it of little value at ranges under 1,300 yards (1,200m). The missile itself weighs 59lbs (26.7kg) and has a single-stage solid-propellant motor which has a burn time of 1.18 seconds. Once the missile leaves the gun/missile-launcher, four fins at the rear of the missile unfold and it is guided to the target by a two-way infra-red command link which eliminates the need for the gunner to estimate the lead and range of the target. A Sheridan normally carried ten missiles and 20 rounds of ammunition, but this mix can be adjusted as required. In addition, 1,000 rounds of 0.5in and 3,080 rounds of 7.62mm ammunition are carried. The Sheridan is provided with a flotation screen, and when erected this enables the vehicle to propel itself across rivers and streams by its tracks. Night-vision equipment is provided as is an NBC system.

The US Army never considered the M551 one of its better tanks and long ago gave up trying to improve it. The 82nd Airborne Division's 3/73rd Armour is the last combat unit to use the ageing M551 because of the need to supply the parachute-landed division with some — if very limited — tank capability. The division's 57 M551 were the first US tanks to arrive in Saudi Arabia during Operation *Desert Shield*. Their involvement in the destruction of General Noriega's Comandancia headquarters in Panama in December 1989 was perhaps the M551's most memorable recent combat operation. A number of vehicles are also used to simulate Soviet armored vehicles at the National Training Centre at Fort Irwin, California.

Below: A pair of the 82nd Airborne Division's Sheridan light tanks take a break from patrolling the desert during Operation *Desert Storm* in early-1991. Primary armament is a single 152mm gun/missile launcher, backed up by one 7.62mm machine-gun and one 0.5in anti-aircraft machine-gun.

Self-Propelled Artillery

Since the 1960s, the US Army has relied on variants of the M109 and M110 self-propelled guns as its standard field artillery pieces in mechanized divisions. They have proved very reliable and were fortunately designed with plenty of scope for

M109A2/A3/A6

Type: Self-propelled howitzer.
Crew: Six (A2/A3); four (A6).
Armament: One 155mm howitzer (A2); one M185 howitzer (A3); one M284 howitzer (A6); one .5in (12.7mm) Browning anti-aircraft machine-gun.
Armor: 0.79in (20mm) maximum (estimated).
Dimensions: Length (including armament) 21ft 8in (6.61m); length (hull) 20ft 6in (6.26m); width 10ft 10in (3.30m); height (including anti-aircraft machine-gun) 10ft 10in (3.30m).
Weight: Combat 55,000lb (24,948kg).
Ground Pressure: 10.95lb/in² (0.77kg/cm²).
Engine: Detroit Diesel Model 8V71T eight-cylinder turbocharged diesel developing 405bhp at 2,300rpm.
Performance: Road speed 35mph (56km/h); range 242 miles (390km); vertical obstacle 1ft 9in (0.53m); trench 6ft (1.83m); gradient 60 per cent.
Range: (A2/A3) 11.24 miles (18.1km) unassisted; 14.6 miles (23.5km) RAP.
History: Entered service with the United States Army in 1963. Also used by Austria, Belgium, Canada, Denmark, Germany, Great Britain, Ethiopia, Greece, Iran, Israel, Italy, Jordan, Kampuchea, Kuwait, Libya, Morocco, the Netherlands, Norway, Oman, Pakistan, Saudi Arabia, Spain, South Korea, Switzerland, Taiwan, Tunisia and Turkey. Still in production.

The first production models of the M109 were completed in 1962, and some 3,700 examples have now been built (of which about 1,800 are in US Army service), making the M109 the most widely used self-propelled howitzer in the world. It has a hull of all-welded aluminum construction, providing the crew with protection from small arms fire. The driver is seated at the front of the hull on the left, with the engine to his right. The other five crew members are the commander, gunner and three ammunition members, all located in the turret at the rear of the hull. There is a large door in the rear of the hull for ammunition resupply purposes. Hatches are also provided in the sides and rear of the turret. There are two hatches in the roof of the turret, the commander's hatch being on the right. A 0.5in (12.7mm) Browning machine-gun is mounted on this for anti-aircraft defense purposes.

The 155mm howitzer has an elevation of +75° and a depression of −3°, and the turret can be traversed through 360°. Elevation and traverse are powered, with manual controls for emergency use. The weapon can fire a variety of ammunition, including HE, tactical nuclear, illuminating, smoke and chemical rounds. Rate of fire is four rounds per minute for three minutes, followed by one round per minute for the next hour. A total of 28 rounds of separate-loading ammunition is carried, as well as 500 rounds of machine-gun ammunition.

The M109 can ford streams to a maximum depth of 6ft (1.828m). A

upgrading. The ageing M110, however, is now being replaced by the MLRS and plans are well advanced to signficantly upgrade the M109.

In the run-up to the Gulf War many pundits said that Iraq's Soviet-made artillery was superior to the American-designed weapons in use with US, British and Arab forces. The devastating combat performance of the M109, M110 and MLRS proved that the Soviet "Gods of War" are not invincible.

Dual-Purpose Improved Conventional Munitions, such as the MLRS rocket, 203mm M509A1 and 155mm M483A1 rounds, which scatter bomblets, increased the lethality of each US artillery round by a factor of seven during the Gulf War.

Above: An M109 155mm self-propelled howitzer doing what it does best — firing projectiles in an arc deep into the enemy's territory. The weapon has an elevation of +75 and the turret can be traversed through a full 360°. The gun's elevation and the turret's traverse are both carried out hydraulically.

special amphibious kit has been developed for the vehicle but this is not widely used. It consists of nine inflatable airbags, normally carried by a truck. Four of these are fitted to each side of the hull and the last to the front of the hull. The vehicle is then propelled in the water by its tracks at a maximum speed of 4mph (6.4km/h). The M109 is provided with infra-red driving lights and some vehicles also have an NBC system.

A continuous improvement program has kept the M109 in the forefront ▶

▶ of artillery technology, with the M109A2/A3 the main version in use today It features a fume extractor, improved shell rammer and recoil mechanism and an M178 modified gun mount. An onboard ballistic computer and navigation system, a new cannon and mount, automotive improvements, driver's night vision capability and an improved NBC system are incorporated in the M109A6 Paladin, which is expected to enter service in 1993.

The introduction of M549A1 rocket-assisted rounds (RAP) has dramatically increased the performance of the M109, boosting the range of the M109A2 to 26,250 yards (23,500m). With the new M284 cannon on the Paladin the M109's range will be further increased to 32,800 yards (30,000m) when RAPs are fired. M687 binary chemical and M785 nuclear rounds can be fired by all versions of the M109.

Right: M109A1 155mm SP howitzer fresh from the production line at the Cleveland Ordnance Plant, run by Cadillac Motor Car Division. This fine weapons system is in service with over 30 armies and has proved a great success.

Below: With their huge guns ranged right, M109A2s wait for the instruction to commence firing. Normal rate of fire is one round per minute; the maximum is four rounds per minute for three minutes, followed by one round per minute for one hour.

M110A2

M110, M110A1, M110A2

Type: Self-propelled howitzer.
Crew: 5 plus 8 (see text).
Armament: One 8in (203mm) howitzer.
Armor: 20mm (0·79in) maximum (estimated).
Dimensions: Length (including gun and spade in traveling position) 35ft 2½in (10·731m); length (hull) 18ft 9in (5·72m); width 10ft 4in (3·149m); height 10ft 4in (3·143m).
Weight: Combat 62,500lb (28,350kg).
Ground pressure: 10·80lb/in² (0·76kg/cm²).
Engine: Detroit Diesel Model 8V-7T eight-cylinder turbo-charged diesel developing 405bhp at 2,300rpm.
Performance: Road speed 34mph (54·7km/h); range 325 miles (523km); vertical obstacle 3ft 4in (1·016m); trench 7ft 9in (2·362m); gradient 60 per cent.
History: Original version, M110, entered service with the United States Army in 1963. Now used by Belgium, West Germany, Greece, Iran, Israel, Japan, Jordan, Saudi Arabia, South Korea, Netherlands, Pakistan, Spain, Turkey, United Kingdom and United States.

In 1956 the United States Army issued a requirement for a range of self-propelled artillery which would be air-transportable. The Pacific Car and Foundry Company of Washington were awarded the development contract and from 1958 built three different self-propelled weapons on the same chassis. These were the T235 (175mm gun), which became the

M107, the T236 (203mm howitzer), which became the M110, and the T245 (155mm gun), which was subsequently dropped from the range. These prototypes were powered by a petrol engine, but it was soon decided to replace this by a diesel engine as this could give the vehicles a much greater range of action. The M107 is no longer in service with the US Army; all have been rebuilt to M110A2 configuration. The M110A2 is also in production by Bowen-McLaughlin-York Company, and when present orders have been completed the US Army wil have a total inventory of over 1,000.

The hull is of all-welded-steel construction with the driver at the front on the left with the engine to his right. The gun is mounted towards the rear of the hull. The suspension is of the torsion-bar type and consists of five road wheels, with the fifth road wheel acting as the idler, the drive sprocket is at the front. Five crew are carried on the gun (driver, commander and three gun crew), the other eight crew members following in an M548 tracked vehicle (this is based on the M113 APC chassis), which also carries the ammunition, as only two ready rounds are carried on the M110 itself. The 203mm howitzer has an elevation of +65° and a depression of −2°, traverse being 30° left and 30° right. Elevation and traverse are both hydraulic, although there are manual controls for use in an emergency. The M110 fires an HE projectile to a maximum range of 26,575 yards (24,300m), and other types of projectile that can be fired include HE carrying 104 HE grenades, HE carrying 195 grenades, Agent GB or VX and tactical nuclear. A large hydraulically-operated spade is mounted at the rear of the hull and is lowered into position before the gun opens fire, and the suspension can also ▶

Below: M110A2 of the US Army. This version has the new M201 cannon which is 8ft (2·44m) longer than that mounted on the M110. The major shortcoming is the lack of a protective gun housing.

be locked when the gun is fired to provide a more stable firing platform. The gun can officially fire one round per two minutes, but a well-trained crew can fire one round per minute for short periods. As the projectile is very heavy, an hydraulic hoist is provided to position the projectile on the ramming tray; the round is then pushed into the breech hydraulically before the charge is pushed home, the breechlock closed and the weapon is then fired. The M110 can ford streams to a maximum depth of 3ft 6in (1.066m) but has no amphibious capability. Infra-red driving lights are fitted as standard but the type does not have a Nuclear, Biological and Chemical (NBC) system.

All M110s in US Army service, and in an increasing number of NATO countries as well, have been brought up to M110A2 configuration. The M110A1 has a new and longer barrel, while the M110A2 is identical to the M110A1 but has a double baffle muzzle brake. The M110A1 can fire up to charge eight while the M110A2 can fire up to charge nine. The

Below: Loading the M110A2, improved version of the Army's heaviest cannon artillery weapon. It has conventional and nuclear capability, firing at a rate of one round per minute.

M110A1/M110A2 can fire all of the rounds of the M110 but in addition binary, high-explosive Rocket Assisted Projectile (M650), and the improved conventional munition which contains 195 M42 grenades. The latter two have a maximum range, with charge nine, of 32,800 yards (30,000m).

The M110A2 also fires the M753 rocket-assisted tactical nuclear round, which entered production in FY 1981. The M753 will be available in two versions: the first as a normal nuclear round; the second as an "Enhanced Radiation" version. These nuclear rounds are packed in very sophisticated containers to prevent unauthorized use and are subject to very stringent controls. The ER rounds will not be deployed outside the USA expect in an emergency.

The M110 203mm gun is showing its age and is slowly being replaced by the MLRS in general support battalions. Few active duty units now use the gun. It saw service in the Gulf War with the 142nd and 196th National Guard Field Artillery Brigades, US Marine Corps artillery regiments and 1st British Armoured Division. The M110's lack of crew protection was a major shortcoming and in the Gulf War they had to quickly move their firing positions on completion of their firing instructions to avoid Iraqi counter-battery fire.

Towed Artillery

In the age of M1A1 Abrams tanks, MLRS rockets and other high-tech weapons, old-fashioned towed artillery pieces may seem an anachronism. Yet these simple weapons are vital to the effectiveness of airportable units and infantry forces expected to fight in jungles or mountainous terrain.

M102

Type: Light howitzer.
Caliber: 105mm.
Crew: 8.
Weight: 3,298lb (1,496kg).
Length firing: 22ft (6.718m).
Length travelling: 17ft (5.182m).
Height firing: 4.29ft (1.308m).
Height travelling: 5.22ft (1.594m).
Width: 6.44ft (1.964m).
Ground clearance: 1.08ft (0.33m).
Elevation: −5° to +75°.
Traverse: 360°.
Range: 12,576 yards (11,500m), standard ammunition; 16,513 yards (15,100m) with RAP.

For over 25 years, the M102 has been the standard weapon of US Army light forces, serving in Vietnam, Grenada, Panama and the Gulf War. Extensive use of aluminum enabled great weight savings to be made and allowed it to be easily dropped by parachute.

A turntable allows for 360° traverse when the gun's wheels are raised off the ground. Anti-tank, anti-personnel, illuminating, smoke, chemical, high explosive, HEP-T and leaflet rounds can be fired. One gun can be underslung on a UH-60A and two can be lifted by a CH-47D.

Below: The M102 has served for many years in the 82nd Airborne Division, for which its light weight and compact dimensions, combined with good stability and all-round traverse make it an ideal weapon. All-up weight is 3,298lb (1,496kg).

While billions of dollars have been invested in heavy-tracked artillery systems, on numerous occasions the US military has learned the worth of cheap guns that can be loaded into a transport plane or slung under a helicopter. Old 105mm M102 howitzers were vital to the success of the 82nd Airborne Division's breakout from the airhead at Point Salines during the invasion of Grenada. The division's Field Artillery Brigade was also the first US artillery unit to arrive in Saudi Arabia in the first days of Operation *Desert Shield* and subsequently proved its worth during Operation *Desert Storm*.

M114A2

Type: Howitzer.
Caliber: 155mm.
Crew: 11.
Weight: 12,700lb (5,761kg).
Length travelling: 23.9ft (7.315m).
Width travelling: 7.99ft (2.438m).
Height travelling: 5.9ft (1.8m).
Elevation: −2° to +63°.
Traverse: 25° right and 24° left.
Range: 21,106 yards (19,300m).

This World War Two-vintage weapon is no longer in service with active duty US Army units. However, Army National Guard and Army Reserve still use the upgraded M114A2 although its days are numbered with the introduction of the new M198 155mm gun. The M114A2 features a new barrel designed for use by the US Marine Corps to allow the standard 155mm round used by the M109 self-propelled gun to be fired.

In its day, the M114 was a superb artillery weapon, seeing service in World War Two, Korea and Vietnam. The gun fires separate loading ammunition (projectile and charge). Rounds including high explosive, tactical nuclear, illuminating and chemical can be fired. When the weapon is in the firing position, it is supported on its two trail legs and a firing jack which is generally a 6x6 truck.

Below: An excellent 155mm howitzer, the M114 has proved itself time and time again in US Army service. Today, the M114A2 is the operational model, this being the designation for M114A1s converted to carry an enhanced cannon to improve firing range.

M119

Type: Towed howitzer.
Caliber: 105mm.
Crew: 7.
Length travelling: 15.8ft (4.8m).
Length firing: 20ft (6.09m).
Width travelling: 5.8ft (1.78m).
Width firing: 5.8ft (1.78m).
Height travelling: 4ft (1.22m).
Elevation: −5.5° to +70°.
Traverse: 360° on platform.
Range: 56,400ft (17,200m).

To replace the ageing M102 the US Army has made an off-the-shelf purchase of British L119 105mm Light Guns. Initial purchases are being made direct from the Royal Ordnance Company to equip the 7th Infantry Division. Subsequent production of more than 200 guns will be carried out in the USA.

The tried-and-tested L119 saw service with the Royal Artillery during the Falklands campaign, and its combat performance in the Battle of Port Stanley greatly impressed US officers involved in choosing a replacement for the M102.

In US service the weapon will be designated the M119, and is intended to replace all M102s in active duty units. The M102s will then be passed on to reserve units to replace the M101s. The M119 can fire all conventional 105mm rounds in the US Army's inventory, as well as DPICM and RAP ammunition. It can also be underslung by UH-60 and CH-47 transport helicopters. The CH-47 can also carry the weapon internally. The HMMWV has been designated as its prime mover.

M198

Type: Towed howitzer.
Caliber: 155mm.
Crew: 10.
Weight: 15,795lb (7,165kg).
Length firing: 37ft 1in (11.302m).
Length traveling: 23ft 3in (7.086m).
Width firing: 28ft (8.534m).
Width traveling: 9ft 2in (2.79m).
Height firing (minimum): 5.91ft (1.803m).
Height traveling: 9.92ft (3.023m).
Ground clearance: 13in (0.23m).
Elevation: −4.2° to +72°.
Traverse: 22.5° left and right; 360° with speed traverse.
Range: 32,808 yards (30,000m) with RAP; 24,060 yards (22,000m) with conventional round.

Designed in the late-1960s to replace the M114 in airborne and light units, the M198 is now in widespread service with the US Army and Marine Corps. The weapon received its combat debut during the deployment of US Marines to Beirut in the mid-1980s. It also served in the Gulf War with the US Marine Corps and the US Army's 18th Field Artillery Brigade. Some 585 are in US Army service and further procurement is not planned.

The M198 has proved to be a rugged and effective weapon during its brief career. While the weapon is airportable in C-130s, C-141s and C-5s, it is too big to be parachuted from any current US transport aircraft. This is a major draw back and prevents the weapon serving with the parachute-

Above: An M198 howitzer firing at its maximum elevation of 72°, a capability necessary to clear crests or to fire out of a jungle.

landed elements of the 82nd Airborne Division.

To tow the M198, its barrel is swung through 180° so that it rests over the trails. The weapon's 82° elevation allows it to fire out of jungle clearings. It uses the full range of US Army 155mm ammunition, including the Copperhead laser-guided round.

Aviation

The US Army is the world's largest operator of military helicopters, with some 8,500 in service alongside more than 600 fixed-wing aircraft. Laser missile-guidance and night vision systems have transformed US Army helicopters from being mere utility transport machines into highly-effective offensive weapon systems.

Beechcraft C-12/U-21

C-12, RC-12, RU-21

Type: Fixed-wing utility aircraft.
Engines: Two 850shp Pratt and Whitney of Canada PT6A-38 (C-12A) turboprops.
Dimensions: Overall length 43.75ft (13.34m); height 15ft (4.57m); wing span 54.5ft (16.61m); wing area 303ft² (28.15m²).
Weights: Gross weight (C-12) 12,500lb (5,670kg), (RC-12) 14,000lb (6,350kg).
Performance: Cruising speed 242 knots (448km/h); range with full payload 1,681 nautical miles (3,115km); mission ceiling (C-12) 31,000ft (9,450m), (RC-12) 27,000ft (8,230m).
History: First flight (Super King Air 200) 27 October 1972; entered service (C-12A) July 1975.

Development: To move key personnel and supplies quickly within its various theatres of operations, the US Army has a fleet of almost 300 light aircraft. Beech Aircraft have provided the majority of these, with 119 C-12s (Super King Air 200) and 117 U-21s (Queen Air 80) currently in service.
　In the early-1970s the US Army started a project, codenamed Guardrail, to

These technologies proved themselves in battle during the Gulf War, when AH-64A Apache attack helicopters armed with Hellfire missiles inflicted devastating damage on the Iraqi Army. The potential of helicopters to move troops around the battlefield has been recognized by the US Army since the Vietnam War, and its airmobile unit — the 101st Airborne Division (Air Assault) — played a key role in Operation *Desert Storm*.

Airborne radar aircraft, such as the OV-ID Mohawk and E-8 Joint STARS, were also stellar performers in the Gulf War.

---

modify U-21s into airborne electronic intelligence-gathering platforms. Designated RU-21G/E/Hs, they served in Vietnam and many were deployed in Germany to monitor the Warsaw Pact's military build-up. The aircraft would operate in pairs to triangulate the location of radio transmitters. Intercepted messages were also transmitted to ground stations for decoding. Starting in 1984, the small RU-21H Guardrail V was replaced in frontline service by the RC-12D Improved Guardrail V, which fields a more capable electronics suite. It is to be replaced in turn by the RC-12H, which is fitted with the Guardrail Common Sensor Minus system. Some utility C-12As were also reported to have been fitted with cameras for covert intelligence-gathering missions while carrying US diplomats over hostile countries. In 1979 the South Africans discovered cameras under the pilot's seat in a C-12A carrying the American ambassador.

The latest version, which is due to enter service in late 1991, is the Guardrail Common Sensor. It is fielded in the RC-12K airframe and its sensor package includes electronic systems interception, classification and direction-finding capabilities. A communications high-accuracy airborne location system (CHAALS) is also fitted. In addition to military applications, Guardrail aircraft are now being deployed for counter-narcotics surveillance.

Below: The standard C-12 transport serves the US Army and the Army National Guard in four versions: C-12A, C, D and F.

Above: Just under one-third of the US Army's fixed-wing fleet is made up of Beech U-21s, 117 of which remain in service. The vast majority in service are militarized Queen Air A90s, but some King Airs/Super King Airs have also been acquired.

Boeing/Grumman E-8A Joint-STARS

Type: Airborne battle management and targetting system.
Detection range: In excess of 62 miles (100km) into hostile territory.
Platform: E-8A (Militarised Boeing 707 airframe).
History: Initial operational field test with ground station conducted in 1990.

Joint-STARS is a joint US Army/USAF programme, with the ground station modules (GSM) and aircrew battle staff being provided by the US Army, while the aircraft and aircrew belong to the USAF. The system combines a powerful airborne radar with computerized data links to enable US Army commanders to monitor in real-time the movement of enemy forces deep behind the front line. Attack aircraft or deep-strike missiles can then be immediately ordered to destroy the enemy positions.

Above: A mass of aerials and antennae identify this as one of the RC-12D Improved Guardrail V battlefield surveillance platforms. Note that the main cabin windows have been covered over to hide from view much of the onboard equipment.

A system of GSMs allows for information from Joint-STARS to be instantaneously distributed to ground-based headquarters. The GSMs are fitted to purpose-built command trucks.

Although still in the early stages of development, two E-8 Joint-STARS aircraft were deployed to support Operation *Desert Storm* by the prime contractors, Grumman Aerospace. They proved highly effective at locating the movement of Iraqi armor and were also deployed to hunt for mobile SCUD missile launchers.

The success of the system has secured continued funding from Congress and it is currently planned to field a fleet of 20 aircraft by the mid-1990s. Some US Army commanders claim that by giving ground forces an instantaneous view of the battlefield, Joint-STARS has revolutionized contemporary warfare in much the same way that the development of radar changed air combat for ever.

Below: One of the star performers during the Gulf War was the E-8A Joint-STARS, the first two prototypes of which provided invaluable real-time intelligence on Iraqi ground movements.

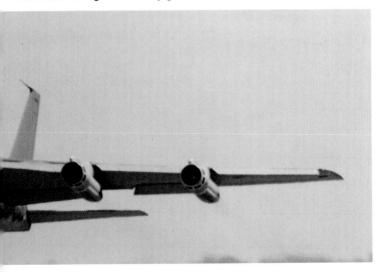

Grumman OV-1 Mohawk

OV-1A to -1D, EV-1, JOV, RV

Type: (OV) multi-sensor tactical observation and reconnaissance; (EV) electronic warfare; (JOV) armed reconnaissance; (RV) electronic reconnaissance.

Engines: Two 1,005shp Lycoming T53-7 or -15 free-turbine turboprops; (OV-1D) two, 1,160shp T53-701.

Dimensions: Span (-1A, -C) 42ft (12·8m); (-1, -D) 48ft (14·63m); length 41ft (12·5m); (-1D with SLAR, 44ft 11in); height 12ft 8in (3·86m).

Weights: Empty (-1A) 9,937lb (4,507kg); (-1B) 11,067lb (5,020kg); (-1C) 10,400lb (4,717kg); (-1D) 12,054lb (5,467kg); maximum loaded (-1A) 15,031lb (6,818kg); (11B, C) 19,230lb (8,722kg); (-1D) 18,109lb (8,214kg).

Performance: Maximum speed (all) 297-310mph (480-500km/h); initial climb (-1A) 2,950ft (900m)/min; (-1B) 2,250ft (716m)/min; (-1C), 2,670ft (814m)/min; (-1D) 3,618ft (1,103m)/min; service ceiling (all) 28,800-31,000ft (8,534-9,449m); range with external fuel (-1A) 1,410 miles (2,270km); (-1B) 1,230 miles (1,980km); (-1C) 1,330 miles (2,140km); (-1D), 1,011 miles (1,627km).

Armament: Not normally fitted, but can include a wide variety of air-to-ground weapons including grenade launchers, Minigun pods and small guided missiles.

History: First flight (YOV-1A) 14 April, 1959; service delivery, February 1961; final delivery (new aircraft) December 1970.

Development: Representing a unique class of military aircraft, the OV-1 Mohawk is a specially designed battlefield surveillance machine with characteristics roughly midway between lightplanes and jet fighters. One of its requirements was to operate from rough forward airstrips and it has exceptional STOL (short takeoff and landing) qualities and good low-speed control with full-span slats and triple fans and rudders. Pilot and observer sit in side-by-side Martin Baker J5 seats and all versions have extremely good all-round view and very comprehensive navigation and communications equipment. All versions carry cameras and upward-firing flares for night photography. Most variants carry UAS-4 infra-red surveillance equipment and the -1B carries APS-94 SLAR (side-looking airborne radar) in a long pod under the right side of the fuselage, with automatic film processing giving, within seconds of exposure, a permanent film record of radar image on either side of the flight path. The -1D combined the functions of the two previous versions in being quickly convertible to either IR or SLAR missions. Underwing pylons can carry 150 US gal drop tanks,

Above: Unglamorous yet highly distinctive in appearance, the OV-1 Mohawk has been an unsung hero of the US Army's observation and electronic intelligence-gathering community for many years. The long, pencil-like radome beneath the starboard forward fuselage houses the AN/APS-94 side-looking airborne radar (SLAR).

Under the *Quick Look I & II* programs they are intended to locate enemy mobile SAM radars. The US Army plans to retire its fleet of 110 OV-1Ds and 36 RV-1Ds by 1997. In 1990, Congress ordered the USAF to transfer OA-10As to the US Army for observation duties, but plans have yet to be announced for converting the tankbusting A-10s into radar platforms. Mohawks were deployed to support Operation *Desert Storm*, their SLAR proving very effective at detecting Iraqi armored formations.

Below: In addition to the prominent AN/APS-94 SLAR, the Mohawk can carry various other forms of intelligence-gathering systems, including optical cameras and an optional UAS-4 IR linescanner. A pair of underwing auxiliary fuel tanks greatly extend the OV-1's mission endurance, allowing it to remain on-station for longer.

McDonnell Douglas AH-64A Apache

Type: Attack helicopter.

Engines: Two 1,696shp General Electric T700-GE-701 turboshafts.

Dimensions: Diameter of four-blade main rotor 48ft 0in (14.64m); length overall (rotors turning) 58ft 3in (17.77m); length of fuselage 49ft 1in (14.97m); height (to top of hub) 15ft 3in (4.67m).

Weights: Empty 10,760lb (4,885kg); mission gross 14,445lb (6,558kg).

Performance: Never-exceed speed 227mph (365km/h); maximum level speed 184mph (296km/h); rate of climb (at sea level) 2,500ft/min (762.5m/min); max range (internal fuel) 300 miles (483km); ferry range (internal and external fuel) 1,057 miles (1,701km).

Armament: Four underwing hardpoints for up to 16 Hellfire missiles or 76 Hydra 70 rockets (or mixture of both); two wingtip hardpoints for Sidewinder or Air-to-Air Stinger missiles; turret under forward fuselage housing one 30mm M230A-1 Chain Gun with 1,200 rounds of varied types of ammunition.

History: First flight (YAH-64) 30 September 1975; initial deliveries (AH-64A) 26 January 1984; IOC (AH-64A) July 1986.

Right: One of the US Army's 600+ AH-64A Apaches looses off a salvo of 2.75in (70mm) folding-fin aerial rockets from each of the two outboard underwing pods. On each of the inner pylons hangs a quartet of AGM-114A Hellfire anti-armor missiles; a weapon that blitzed Iraqi armor over and over during Operation *Desert Storm*.

Below: Banking away hard from the camera-ship, an Apache gives a clear demonstration of its excellent maneuverability, and at the same time reveals yet another formidable weapon: the 30mm M230A-1 Chain Gun. Located under the forward fuselage, it is designed to collapse upwards during a crash-landing.

▶ After taking a heavy battering from Congress because of its long and expensive development, the Apache emerged from the Gulf War as one of the US Army's greatest performers. Apaches led the US Army's ground offensive into Iraq, destroying tanks, artillery and bunkers that threatened to block the Allies' advance. Initial Apache "kill" claims ran to 500 tanks, 120 APCs, 30 air defence sites, 120 artillery pieces, 325 trucks, 50 bunkers, 10 helicopters and 10 aircraft hit on the ground. Apaches also assisted directly in the capture of 4,500 POWs.

The US Army deployed 278 Apaches — 15 battalions worth — to Saudi Arabia. Readiness rates in excess of peacetime levels were reported throughout Operation *Desert Storm*, confounding critics who said the complex Apache would be crippled by the harsh desert conditions.

Central to the Apache's success was it TADS/PNVS sensor suite, which allows the helicopter to fly and fight at night and in bad weather. Much effort has gone into ensuring the Apache's survivability on the battlefield. It is fitted with a full suite of anti-missile defence systems, such as passive radar warning receivers and IR jammers. In addition, the crew compartment and other key areas of the helicopters are protected by Kevlar armor and electro-slag remelt steel.

The first Apache entered US Army service in December 1981 and 582 had been delivered by April 1990. Current plans call for production of the AH-64A to end after the delivery of 132 funded in the 1990 budget. The US Army's helicopter fleet will then boast some 807 Apaches. An upgrading program is underway to fit the LONGBOW millimeter-wave radar system to allow the "fire-and-forget" Advanced Hellfire missile to be fired. Some 227 Apaches are to be upgraded to LONGBOW standard.

Below: When it comes to nap-of-the-earth flying, using terrain as a natural form of cover, the Apache is in its element.

Above: The latest variant is the Longbow Apache, complete with a 300lb (136kg) millimeter-wave radar atop the main rotor.

Bell AH-1S/F HueyCobra

Type: Attack helicopter.
Engine: 1,800shp Lycoming T53-L-703 turboshaft.
Dimensions: Main-rotor diameter 44ft (13.4m); overall length (rotors turning) 52ft 11½in (16.14m); length of fuselage 44ft 5in (13.54m); height 13ft 5½in (4.1m).
Weights: Empty 6,598lb (2,993kg); maximum 10,000lb (4,536kg).
Performance: Maximum speed (TOW configuration) 141mph (227km/h); max rate of climb (SL, rated power) 1,620ft (494m)/min; service ceiling (rated power) 12,200ft (3.719m); hovering ceiling in ground effect, same; range (max fuel, SL, 8% reserve) 315 miles (507km).
Armament: M65 system with nose telescope sight and crew helmet sights for cueing and guiding eight TOW missiles on outboard underwing pylons; chin turret (to 100th AH-1S) M28 with 7.62mm Minigun and 40mm M129 grenade launcher with 300 bombs, (from No. 101) GE Universal turret with 20mm M197 three-barrel gun (or alternative 30mm); also wide range of cluster/fuel-air explosive and other weapons or five types of rocket.

Development: First flown in 1965 after only six months of development, the HueyCobra is a combat development of the UH-1 Iroquois family. It combines the dynamic parts — engine, transmission, and rotor system — of the original Huey with a new streamlined fuselage providing for a gunner in the front and pilot above and behind him and for a wide range of fixed and power-aimed armament systems.

The first version of this potent attack helicopter was the US Army AH-1G, which saw extensive service in Vietnam armed with a 7.62mm Mini-gun nose turret and unguided rockets. To give the Cobra an anti-armor capability the AH-1Q, armed with 8 TOW missiles, was brought into service during the 1970s. For most of the 1980s the AH-1S was the definitive US Army Cobra model, and it appeared in four main configurations. The Mod AH-1S' were upgraded AH-1G/Qs; the Production AH-1S had a flat canopy and composite rotors; Up-gun AH-1S' featured a 20mm long barrelled cannon; and the Modernized AH-1S included a laser range finder and sight package. TOW missiles were standard to all AH-1S models. In 1988 the US Army rationalized the designation of its Cobras and the Production version became the AH-1P; the Up-gun was redesignated the AH-1E; and the Modernized Cobras were termed AH-1F. Further developments are under consideration to give the AH-1F a night attack capability and the ability to fire Hellfire missiles.

Above: An AH-1S fires a TOW anti-tank missile. The Cobra/TOW combination can destroy enemy tanks at up to 4,100yds (3,750m).

Above: The pilot's cockpit with its profusion of analogue dials and instruments shows the 1960s origin of the Cobra, although it is set to serve with the US Army into the next century.

Left: The AH-1S introduced the flat-plate canopy to reduce the chance of glint revealing the helicopter in an ambush position.

Boeing Vertol
CH-47D Chinook

Type: Medium transport helicopter.
Engines: Two 3,750shp Lycoming T55-L-11A free-turbine turboshafts.
Dimensions: Diameter of main rotors 60ft (18·29m); length, rotors turning, 99ft (30·2m); length of fuselage 51ft (15.54m); height 18ft 7in (5·67m).
Weights: Empty 20,616lb (9,351kg); loaded (condition 1) 33,000lb (14,969kg); (overload condition II) 46,000lb (20,865kg).
Performance: Maximum speed (condition I) 189mph (304km/h); (II) 142mph (229km/h); initial climb (I) 2,880ft (878m)/min; (II) 1,320ft (402m)/min; service ceiling (I) 15,000ft (4,570m); (II) 8,000ft (2,440m); mission radius, cruising speed and payload (I) 115 miles (185km) at 158mph (254km/h) with 7,262lb (3,294kg); (II) 23 miles (37km) at 131mph (211mph (211km/h) with 23,212lb (10,528kg).
Armament: Normally none.
History: First flight (YCH-47A) 21 September 1961, (CH-47C) 14 October 1967, (D) 11 May 1979.

▶

Above: The CH-47D Chinook's relatively spacious main cabin can accommodate between 33 and 55 combat-equipped troops.

Left: Up to seven 416 gallon (1,893l) rubber fuel blivets can be lifted by a CH-47D in a single transport mission.

Below: A CH-47C delivers an M102 105mm light howitzer, a load well within its capabilities. The CH-47D has three cargo hooks.

Development: Development of the Vertol 114 began in 1956 to meet the need of the US Army for a turbine-engined all-weather cargo helicopter able to operate effectively in the most adverse conditions of altitude and temperature. Retaining the tandem-rotor configuration, the first YCH-47A flew on the power of two 2,200shp Lycoming T55 turboshaft engines and led directly to the production CH-47A. With an unobstructed cabin 7½ft (2.29m) wide, 6½ft (1.98m) high and over 30ft (9.2m) long, the Chinook proved a valuable vehicle, soon standardized as US Army medium helicopter and deployed all over the world. By 1972 more than 550 had served in Vietnam, mainly in the battlefield airlift of troops and weapons but also rescuing civilians (on one occasion 147 refugees and their belongings were carried to safety in one Chinook) and lifting back for salvage or repair 11,500 disabled aircraft valued at more than $3,000 million. The A model gave way to the CH-47B, with 2,850hp engines and numerous improvements.

To save the massive costs involved in developing a new heavylift helicopter, the US Army began a rolling program in 1979 to extend the life of its CH-47A, B and C models beyond the year 2000. The conversion of 472 Chinooks to CH-47D standard is currently underway, with some 270 examples already in service by 1991.

The modernization includes glass-fiber rotor blades, new transmission

Above: A flight of Chinooks demonstrates how outsize loads are carried beneath the aircraft. Each truck is hung by a two-point cargo suspension system which prevents the load spinning and keeps it in a stable, safe position. The Chinook gives operational commanders the flexibility to supply mobile formations with ammunition, fuel and equipment by air, along with the ability to rapidly deploy large numbers of troops.

and drive systems, modularized hydraulics, upgraded electrical systems, advanced flight controls, a triple cargo hook system and an auxiliary power unit. Payloads of up to 24,000lb (10,886kg) can be carried. The US Army plans to purchase a further 26 MH-47Es for its Special Operations Forces. This version is fitted with an air-to-air refuelling probe and night flying sensors for long-range missions behind enemy lines.

Chinooks provided vital logistic support for Operation *Desert Storm*, carrying supplies forward to tank units during the advance into Iraq. They were also used to set up forward supply bases deep inside Iraq for airmobile and attack helicopter units. On a number of occasions CH-47s came under Iraqi surface-to-air missile attack, but none were lost thanks to the fitting of extensive missile countermeasures equipment.

Sikorsky UH-60A Black Hawk

UH-60A, EH-60A

Type: (UH) combat assault transport, (EH) electronic warfare and target acquisition.

Engines: (UH, EH) two 1,560shp General Electric T700-700 free-turbine turboshafts.

Dimensions: Diameter of four-blade rotor 53ft 8in (16·36m); length overall (rotors turning) 64ft 10in (19·76m); length (rotors/tail folded) 41ft 4in (12·6m); height overall 16ft 10in (5·13m).

Weights: Empty 10,624lb (4,819kg); maximum loaded 20,250lb (9,185kg) (normal mission weight 16,260lb, 7,375kg).

Performance: Maximum speed, 184mph (296km/h); cruising speed 167mph (269km/h); range at max wt, 30 min reserves, 373 miles (600km).

Armament: (UH) provision for two M60 LMGs firing from side of cabin, plus chaff/flare dispensers; (EH) electronic only.

History: First flight (YUH) 17 October 1974, (production UH) October 1978, service delivery (UH) June 1979.

Development: The UH-60 was picked in December 1976 after four years of competition with Boeing Vertol for a UTTAS (utility tactical transport aircraft system) for the US Army. Designed to carry a squad of 11 equipped troops and a crew of three, the Black Hawk can have eight troop seats replaced by four litters (stretchers), and an 8,000lb (3,628kg) cargo load can be slung externally. The titanium/glassfibre/Nomex honeycomb rotor is electrically de-iced, as are the pilot windscreens, and equipment includes comprehensive navaids, communications and radar warning. Deliveries to the 101st Airborne Division took place in 1979-81, followed by a further ▶

Right: A UH-60A Black Hawk is off-loaded from a C-5 at Cairo West airport after flying in from the USA on a RDF exercise.

Below: In their true element a group of UH-60s collecting troops from an ad hoc landing zone in scrubland, during an exercise in the USA.

block of 100 to the 82nd Division in 1981. Just over 1,000 Blackhawks are now in service with the US Army. Plans to field over 2,000 examples have been scaled down because of budget cuts and only some 1,447 are now in the US Army's procurement program. Under long-term plans it is intended to provide the Army National Guard with 300 UH-60s in the mid-1990s. The Special Operations MK-60K is due to enter service in 1992 and is fitted with an in-flight refuelling probe and night flying system and some 66 EH-60A "Quickfix" Blackhawks were in service in 1991 for radio interception, direction-finding and jamming work.

The latest production version is the UH-60L, which features a more durable gearbox and a more powerful engine, the new T700-GE-701C. During Operation *Desert Shield* Blackhawks in the Middle East accumluated over 6,000 flight hours in a wide variety of transport-related roles.

Right: The Blackhawk can carry up to 8,000lb (3,628kg) of cargo slung externally beneath the fuselage.

Below: The ability to allow four soldiers to descend by rope at the same time greatly reduces the vulnerable period in the hover.

Bell UH-1 Iroquois

Type: Utility helicopter.

Engine: Originally, one Lycoming T53 free-turbine turboshaft rated at 600-640shp, later rising in stages to 825, 930, 1,100 and 1,400shp; (212) 1,800shp P&WC PT6T-3 (T400) coupled turboshafts, flat-rated at 1,250shp and with 900shp immediately available from either following failure of the other turboshaft.

Dimensions: Diameter of twin-blade main rotor (204, UH-1B, C) 44ft 0in (13.41m), (205,212) 48ft 0in (14.63m) (tracking tips, 48ft 2¼in, 14.69m); (214) 50ft 0in (15.24m); overall length (rotors turning) (early) 53ft 0in (16.15m), (virtually all modern versions) 57ft 3¼in (17.46m); height overall (modern, typical) 14ft 4¾in (4.39m).

Weights: Empty (XH-40) about 4,000lb (1,814kg), (typical 205) 4,667lb (2,110kg), (typical 212) 5,549lb (2,517kg); maximum loaded (XH-40) 5,800lb (2,631kg), (typical 205) 9,500lb (4,309kg), (212/UH-1N) 10,500lb (4,762kg).

Performance: Maximum speed (all) typically 127mph (204km/h); econ cruise speed, usually same; max range with useful payload, typically 248 miles (400km).

Armament: See text.

History: First flight (XH-40) 22 October 1956, (production UH-1) 1958, (205) August 1961, (212) 1969.

Development: Used by more air forces, and built in greater numbers, than any other military aircraft since World War II, the "Huey" family of helicopters grew from a single prototype, the XH-40, for the US Army. Over 20 years, the gross weight has been multiplied by almost three, though the size has changed only slightly. Early versions seated eight to ten, carried the occasional machine-gun, and included the TH-1L Seawolf trainer for the US Navy. Prior to 1962 the Army/Navy designation was basically HU-1, which gave rise to the name Huey, though the (rarely used) official name

Below: The classic airmobile mission. These troopers from the 1st Cavalry (Airmobile) Division deploy from a UH-1D during Operation *Oregon* in the Vietnam War.

Above: The UH-1 series has been built in greater numbers than any other military aircraft since World War II.

is Iroquois. Since 1962 the basic designation has officially been UH-1 (utility helicopter type 1).

In August 1961 Bell flew the first Model 205 with many changes of which the greatest was a longer fuselage giving room for up to 14 passengers or troops, or six litters (stretchers) and an attendant, or up to 3,880lb (1,759kg) of cargo. All versions have blind-flying instruments, night lighting, FM/VHF/UHF radios, IFF transponder, DF/VOR, powered controls, and searchlight. Options include a hook for a slung load, rescue hoist, and various fits of simple weapons or armor.

Some 3,200 UH-1Hs are in US Army service and most of them are expected to continue in use until well into the next century. A specialist electronic warfare (EW) version, the EH-1H, has been developed, with some 20 examples in service.

To keep its UH-1Hs up to modern standards a program was initiated in the mid-1980s to retro-fit the US Army's "Hueys" with glass-fiber composite rotor blades, radar warning receivers, IR jammers and other avionics improvements. Today, the Huey has all but disappeared from frontline aviation assault companies and now serves largely in support roles, such as casualty evacuation and logistics. A disproportiate number of the UH-1Hs now serve in US Army reserve units.

Below: The ubiquitous "Huey" has seen extensive service with dozens of air arms in all climatic and geographic conditions. This US Army example is performing as an airborne command post, hovering above an M577 armored command vehicle during a desert exercise in the Continental United States.

Bell OH-58C/D Kiowa Warrior

Type: Light observation helicopter/Army Helicopter Improvement Program (AHIP).

Engine: (OH-58A, TH-57A) one 317shp Allison T63-700 turboshaft, (OH-58C) 420shp T63-720, (OH-58D) 650shp 250-C30R..

Dimensions: Diameter of two-blade main rotor 35ft 4in (10.77m); length overall (rotors turning) 40ft 11¾in (12.49m); height 9ft 6½in (2.91m); skid track 6ft 2in (1.88m).

Weights: Empty (C) 1,585lb (719kg), (D) 2,825lb (1,281kg); maximum (C) 3,200lb (1,451kg), (D) 4,500lb (2,041kg).

Performance: Maximum speed 139mph (224km/h); service ceiling (C) 19,000ft (5.791m); range (SL, no weapons, 10% reserve) 299 miles (481km).

Armament: See text.

History: First flight (OH-4A) 8 December 1962, (206A) 10 January 1966, (production OH-58C) 1978, (AHIP) 6 October 1983.

Below: The AHIP development of the OH-58 is an extremely effective light attack and reconnaissance machine. The mast-mounted sight is fully stabilized and carries TV, infra-red and laser sensors. Hellfire and Stinger missiles can be carried, as can a range of gun pods and unguided rockets.

Development: The loser in the US Army Light Observation Helicopter contest of 1962, the 206 was marketed as the civil JetRanger, this family growing to encompass the more powwerful 206B and more capacious 206L LongRanger. In 1968 the US Army re-opened the LOH competition, naming Bell as the winner and buying 2,200 OH-58A Kiowas, similar to the 206A but with larger main rotor.

During the 1980s, the OH-58C Kiowa was the standard model and featured an uprated engine, flat-plate canopy to reduce glint, new instrument panel and avionics improvements. Standard armament was a 7.62mm Mini-gun on a mounting just behind the port cabin door.

The US Army has been systematically improving the capability of the OH-58, with a major rebuilding program beginning in 1981. Termed AHIP (Army Helicopter Improvement Program), almost 280 helicopters have been brought up to OH-58D Kiowa Warrior standard, with a more powerful T63-type engine (650hp), a new four-blade rotor, mounts for four Hellfire missiles and a mast-mounted sensor ball for TV and FLIR laser ranger/designators. A further modification has been made to allow the OH-58D to fire the Air-to-Air Stinger missile.

Attack, air cavalry and artillery units used the OH-58D to great effect to locate targets during the Gulf War. Successful designation for Copperhead laser-guided artillery rounds, USAF laser-guided bombs and Hellfire missiles launched from Apaches was commonplace. Iraqi patrol boats and oil platforms were succesfully engaged with the OH-58D's own Hellfires.

McDonnell Douglas OH-6 Cayuse/MH-6 Little Bird

Type: Light observation helicopter.
Engine: One Allison turboshaft T63-5A flat-rated at 252.5shp.
Dimensions: Diameter of four-blade main rotor 26ft 4in (8.03m); length overall (rotors turning) 30ft 3¼in (9.24m); height overall 8ft 1½in (2.48m).
Weights: Empty 1,229lb (557kg), maximum loaded 2,700lb (1,225kg).
Performance: Max cruise at S/L 150mph (241km/h); typical range on normal fuel 380 miles (611km).
Armament: See text.
History: First flight (OH-6A) 27 February 1963.

Development: Original winner of the controversial LOH (Light Observation Helicopter) competition of the US Army in 1961, the OH-6A Cayuse is one of the most compact flying machines in history, relative to its capability. The standard machine carries two crew and four equipped troops, or up to 1,000lb (454kg) of electronics and weapons including the XM-27 gun or XM-75 grenade launcher plus a wide range of other infantry weapons. The US Army bought 1,413 and several hundred other military or paramilitary examples have been built by Hughes or its licensees. The Cayuse, or Loach, as it is known by US Army aviators, now serves mainly in Army National Guard units. Although an armed version failed to win the US

Boeing/Sikorsky RAH-66 Commanche

Type: Light scout/attack helicopter.
Engines: Two 1,200shp LHTec T800 turboshafts.
Dimensions: Length 43.3ft (13.3m); width 7.5ft (2.28m); height 11.02ft (3.4m); rotor diameter 39ft (11.89m).
Weights: Empty 7,500lb (3,401kg).
Performance: 196mph (315km/h).
Armament: Hellfire and Stinger anti-tank missiles; 70 2.75in (70mm) rockets; one 20mm turret-mounted cannon firing at 750 or 1,500 rounds-per-minute (airborne or ground targets).
History: Research work started in 1983. Selected in April 1991.

The Boeing/Sikorsky "First Team" design won the US Army's Light Helicopter (LH) contest against McDonnell Douglas/Bell's "Super Team" design in April 1991 to provide 1,292 light scout/attack helicopters. Named the Commanche, the RAH-66 is intended to replace the US Army's OH-58s, AH-1s and OH-6s in the armed reconnaissance role. Current plans call for the first RAH-66 to enter service in 1998.
  Advanced sensor and targetting systems are to be linked to a helmet which can generate visual displays. Highly advanced targetting systems will be able to designate targets for AH-64s, artillery and USAF precision-guided munitions. The Commanche employs the advanced FANTAIL rotor system, which protects the helicopters tail rotors inside the fuselage. Special consideration has been given in the design to strategic movement by USAF transport aircraft, so the helicopter is designed to be rapidly broken down and reconstructed with minimum engineering support.
Boeing/Sikorsky say their helicopter will cost $8.9 million per copy. The full-scale development and prototype phase contracts are worth $2.5 billion. Overall programme costs are expected to exceed $40 billion.

Above: A stalwart performer within the US Army's rotary-winged fleet for some 30 years, the OH-6's days are now numbered.

Army's AHIP programme, some have entered service with the highly secretive 160th Special Operations Aviation Regiment under the designation MH-6 Little Bird. They saw service during the Persian Gulf Tanker War in the mid-1980s, when their low noise and heavy armament was very effective against armed Iranian speed boats. Two were lost in Operation *Just Cause* while supporting *Delta Force* operations againat Panamanian resistance.

Above: An artistic impression of the RAH-66 Commanche (in an earlier incarnation), winner of the US Army's LH competition, as it carries out an attack sortie with anti-armor missiles.

Remotely Piloted Vehicles (RPV)

While the USAF made great use of RPV's during the Vietnam War and the Israelis demonstrated their effectiveness in the 1982 Lebanon invasion, the US Army has yet to field an American-designed operational system.

Pioneer

Type: Remotely piloted vehicle (RPV).
Fuselage length: 14ft (4.26m).
Wing span: 16.9ft (5.15m).
Weights: Total system 419lbs (190kg); payload 100lb (45.35kg).
Performance: 5.5 hour endurance, maximum speed 115mph (185km/h), cruise speed 92mph (148kph); maximum altitude 15,000ft (4,572m).
History: Developed by Israel Aircraft Industries, produced in US by AAI Corp.

Budgetary and technical reasons have delayed US Army RPV efforts over the past decade. The US Army's top brass have never given RPV's much priority and the lead services in their development are the US Navy and Marine Corps. They decided to go for an off-the-shelf purchase in 1988 and bought a number of Israeli-designed Pioneer systems.

The success of Israeli RPV operations in Lebanon and early reports from Operation *Desert Storm* indicate that they are revolutionizing battlefield surveillance and artillery target spotting. Commanders are now able to target stand-off weapons by using "live" video links to RPVs.

To give the US Army an interim RPV capability until a purpose-built system can be brought into service, the service followed the US Navy and Marine Corps' example and formed an unmanned aerial vehicle platoon to carry out training and development work at Fort Huachua, Arizona.

Below: The dramatic launch of an Israeli-built Mazlat Pioneer RPV. Equipment for its reconnaissance mission is housed within the fuselage body, with a transparent viewing panel for cameras an option for US Army operations.

Television and FLIR sensors on the Pioneer can feed back images to a ground station over a range of 100 nautical miles (185.32km). Pioneers can be launched from improvised strips or a twin rail launcher.

The US Army deployed its platoon to Saudi Arabia and it went into action with VII Corps in Operation *Desert Storm*. Five aircraft served with the platoon during the Gulf War, locating targets for artillery and air strikes. They were also employed to provide route reconnaissance for AH-64 Apache attack helicopters. The pilots would watch imagery from the Pioneers before missions and then plan their approach routes to targets. Other Pioneers served with the US Marine Corps, locating targets for the big guns of the battleships USS *Missouri* and *Wisconsin*. On one occasion, Iraqi troops even tried to surrender to a Marine Corps Pioneer! Out of the 2 Pioneers in the Middle East, seven were lost in action. No US Army Pioneers were lost during the campaign.

Right: An autopilot controls the Pioneer RPV from its take-off until it lands. Here, one of these remarkable reconnaissance platforms demonstrates another string to its bow — entrapment in a vertically-strung retrieval net at the end of the sortie.

Below: Israel has led the way in the advancement of the RPV as a credible reconnaissance platform with military applications, and the US Army (along with other US armed services) has been an eager recipient of this compact yet versatile system.

Theater Rockets And Missiles

With the Cold War in Europe thawing, the US Army is finding it increasingly difficult to justify massive investments in so-called tactical nuclear missiles. Already the controversial Pershing II

Lance, MGM-52C

Type: Battlefield support missile.
Dimensions: Length 20ft 3in (6.17m); body diameter 22in (56cm).
Launch weight: 2,833 to 3,367lb (1,285-1,527kg) depending on warhead.
Propulsion: Rocketdyne P8E-9 storable-liquid two-part motor with infinitely throttleable sustainer portion.
Guidance: Simplified inertial.
Range: 45 to 75 miles (70-120km) depending on warhead.
Flight speed: Mach 3.
Warhead: M234 468lb (212kg, 10kT) nuclear, or Honeywell M251, 1,000lb (454kg) high-explosive cluster.

In service since 1972, this neat rocket replaced the earlier Honest John rocket and Sergeant ballistic missile, with very great gains in reduced system weight, cost and bulk and increases in accuracy and mobility. Usual vehicle is the M752 (M113 family) amphibious tracked launcher, with the M688 carrying two extra missiles and a loading hoist. For air-dropped operations a lightweight towed launcher can be used. In-flight guidance accuracy, with the precisely controlled sustainer and spin-stabilization, is already highly satisfactory, but a future missile could have DME (Distance Measuring Equipment) command guidance. The US Army has eight battalions, six of which are deployed in Europe with six launchers each; the two remaining

Below: US Army soldiers transferring a Lance missile from the loader-transporter vehicle (in the background) to the launch vehicle (in the foreground). At 20ft 3in (6.17m) in length and with a diameter of just 22in (56cm), Lance is a quite compact missile. Various warheads, including nuclear and high-explosive, can be carried.

missiles have been bargained away in the Intermediate Nuclear Forces (INF) Treaty process with the Soviet Union.

Plans to upgrade the Lance system have been quietly dropped after NATO members refused to go ahead with what they considered to be a "provocative" program.

The US Army is now focusing its efforts on using highly accurate rocket systems, such as MLRS and Army Tactical Missile System (ATMS), to transform the conventional battlefield. Such weapons inflicted massive casualties on Iraqi troop formations during the Gulf War.

Above: A dramatic study of a Lance missile at the moment of launch. The flames and white smoke come from the Rocketdyne P8E-9 rocket motor, while the plumes of black smoke from the missile's upper body are produced by spin motors. Such a sight will soon be a thing of the past, as Lance missiles fall victim to US defense cuts.

battalions are at Fort Sill, Oklahoma. Lance production lasted from 1971 to 1980, during which time 2,133 missiles were built.

Development of future versions of the Lance missile has been cancelled because of the collapse of the Warsaw Pact. The transformation of the military situation in Europe has totally undermined the rationale for the missile and many NATO countries are looking to retire their Lance batteries. US Army units are likely to be retired by the end of 1992.

No Lance missiles were deployed to the Middle East during Operations *Desert Shield/Desert Storm* because the system's nuclear role made it politically sensitive.

MLRS

Type: Multiple-launch rocket system.
Dimensions: (Rocket) length 13ft (3.96m); diameter 8.94in (227mm).
Launch weight: (Rocket) 600lb (272kg).
Propulsion: Atlantic Research solid rocket motor.
Range: Over 18.6 miles (30km).
Flight speed: Just supersonic.
Warhead: Dispenses payload of sub-munitions, initially 644 standard M77 bomblets.

US Gulf War commanders described it as a "War-Winning" weapon, but ordinary Coalition soldiers were more blunt and called the MLRS' "grid square removers" because of the ability to totally devastate a 1km square area. Iraqis who were on the receiving end of MLRS bombardments called them "Black Rain".

This outstanding weapon system was first fielded by the US Army in 1983, after a nine-year development period. It combines mobility and armored protection with a long reach, high accuracy and very destructive warheads. The M270 armored launch vehicle is based on the M2/M3 Bradley IFV chassis, so it has the same mobility as the armored formations it is designed to support.

Below: An MLRS rocket at the moment of launch. The rocket is 13ft (3.96) long and 8.94in (227mm) in diameter, weighing 600lb (272kg).

Above: MLRS vehicle with launch platform in the travelling position. Note the two rocket containers, each with six pre-loaded tubes.

Previous pages: After moving from its hide to a pre-planned firing position, an MLRS conducts a spectacular night-time launch.

A computer fire control system which includes a GPS satellite navigation suite allows the MLRS's 12 rockets to be targetted in under a minute with pin-point accuracy. Three types of rockets can be fired by the launcher. MLRS1 contains 644 M77 anti-personnel/material bomblets. Some 5,000 of these were fired during the Gulf War against high-value targets such

Army TACMS

Type: Army Tactical Missile System (TACMS).
Dimensions: Length 13ft (4m); diameter 23in (0.6m).
Range: 36 miles (60km) + (Block 1); 99-105 miles (160-170km) (Block 2).
Flight speed: Classified.
Warheads: Submunitions dispenser containing 950 M74 anti-personnel/anti-material bomblets (Block 1) or 26 infra-red terminally-guided anti-tank submuntions (IRTGMS).

Army TACMS supplements the MLRS and provides corps and theater commanders with a highly accurate and destructive deep-strike capability against air defense sites, logistics centers, communications equipment and troop formations. It is fired from a modified M270 MLRS launch vehicle. To give the system a deep strike anti-armor capability, Block 2 missiles are under development.

Block 1 missiles entered low-rate initial production in 1989 and went in full production at LTV's Dallas plant in 1991. US Central Command asked in January 1991 for all the 105 available TACMS to be deployed to Saudi Arabia to deal with critical air-defense and deep theatre targets. VII Corps Artillery fired more than 30 Block 1 missiles at targets in excess of 43 miles (70km) range with great effect. Targets included surface-to-air missile sites, logistics centers, Scud firing sites, artillery and tactical bridges. The system's computerised targetting system is not yet fully operational so targetting information had to be entered manually during the Gulf War, which considerably reduced its rapid response capability.

Above: MLRS ready to fire. The tracked launcher is derived from the Bradley M2 IFV and has similar cross-country capabilities.

as Iraqi artillery, air defense positions, command and control centers and logistic facilities. MLRS2 scatters 28 AT-2 anti-tank mines and is intended to slow the advance of tank formations. MLRS3 is intended to be a precision tank killer and contains three terminally-guided submunitions. The US Army currently fields almost 400 MLRS units.

Above: Fired from a modified M270 MLRS launcher, TACMS consists of a surface-to-surface semi-guided ballistic missile armed with an anti-personnel/anti-material (AP/AM) warhead. The system uses targetting systems, engagement systems, and command and control systems as per the MLRS.

Mortars

Mortars are known in most armies as "the battalion commander's artillery", since they are the major fire support asset under his direct command. Mortars provide a very effective means of bringing heavy fire to bear both speedily and accurately, while their light weight and simplicity of operation make them ideal weapons for the infantry. Unlike

M29A1

Type: Mortar.
Caliber: 81mm.
Weight of barrel: 27·99lb (12·7kg).
Weight of baseplate: 24·91lb (11·3kg).
Weight of bipod: 40lb (18·15kg).
Total weight with sight: 115lb (52·2kg).
Elevation: +40° to +85°.
Traverse: 4° left and 4° right.
Maximum range: 5,140 yards (4,700km).
Rate of fire: 30rpm for 1 minute; 4-12rpm sustained.

In service with US Army and some Allied countries, the 81mm M29 mortar is the standard medium mortar of the US Army and is in service in two basic models, infantry and self-propelled. The standard infantry model can be disassembled into three components, each of which can be carried by one man—baseplate, barrel, mount and sight. The exterior of the barrel is helically grooved both to reduce weight and to dissipate heat when a high rate of fire is being achieved.

The mortar is also mounted in the rear of a modified member of the M113 APC family called the M125A1. In this vehicle the mortar is mounted on a turntable and this enables it to be traversed quickly through 360° to be laid onto a new target. A total of 114 81mm mortar bombs are carried in the vehicle.

The mortar can fire a variety of mortar bombs including HE (the M374 bomb has a maximum range of 5,025 yards (4,595m)), white phosphorus (the M375 bomb has a maximum range of 5,180 yards (4,737m)) and illuminating (the M301 bomb has a maximum range of 3,444 yards (3,150m)). The 81mm M29 has been replaced in certain units by the new M224 60mm Lightweight Company Mortar.

M224

Type: Lightweight company mortar.
Caliber: 60mm.
Total weight: 46lb (20·9kg); (hand-held with M8 baseplate) 17lb (7·7kg).
Maximum range: 3,828 yards (3,500m).

During the Vietnam campaign, it was found that the standard 81mm M29 mortar was too heavy for the infantry to transport in rough terrain, even when disassembled into its three main components. In its place the old 60mm M19 mortar was used, but this had a short range. The M224 has been developed to replace the 81mm M29 mortar in non-mechanized the Soviet Army, however, the US Army has done away with the larger caliber mortars and when the M252 81mm replaces the 4·2in (106mm) in a few years time it will be the largest in US service. This mortar is of British design (the ML L16, with a Canadian-designed baseplate of forged aluminum and the Canadian C2 sight) and was very successfully combat tested in the British campaign in the Falklands in 1982. Its total weight is some 78lb (35·4kg) and it can be broken down into three man-portable loads of about equal weight. Technology is unlikely to produce any major breakthroughs in mortars, although work on the ammunition has led to significant increases in range.

---

infantry, airmobile and airborne units at company level, and is also issued to the US Marine Corps. The weapon comprises a lightweight finned barrel, sight, M7 baseplate and bipod, although if required it can also be used with the lightweight M8 baseplate, in which case it is hand-held. The complete mortar weighs only 46lb (20·9kg) compared to the 81mm mortar which weighs 115 (52kg). The M224 fires an HE bomb which provides a substantial portion of the lethality of the 81mm mortar with a waterproof "horseshoe" snap-off, propellant increments, and the M734 multi-option fuze. This new fuze is set by hand and gives delayed detonation, impact, near-surface burst (0-3ft, 0-0·9m), or proximity burst (3-13ft, 0·9-3·96m).

The mortar can be used in conjunction with the AN/GVS-5 hand held laser rangefinder, this can range up to 10,936 yards (10,000m) to an accuracy of ±10·936 yards (±10m). This enables the mortar to engage a direct-fire target without firing a ranging bomb first. The M224 fires a variety of mortar bombs to a maximum range of 3,828 yards (3,500m) and is currently in production at Watervliet Arsenal. The Army has ordered 1,590 of these mortars while the Marine Corps has ordered 698.

Below: The thirty-year-old M29 mortar is gradually being replaced by the M224 60mm mortar in dismounted infantry units.

Air Defense Weapons

The US Army's air defense arm suffered greatly during the 1980s from lack of funds and development problems with new equipment, such as the ill-fated Sgt. York gun system and Roland surface-to-air missile. Both these systems were eventually scrapped after long and expensive development programs failed to generate weapons systems that actually

Chaparral, M48

Type: Forward area air-defense missile system.
Dimensions: Length 114.5in (2.91m); body diameter 5.0in (12.7cm); span 25in (64cm).
Launch weight: 185lb (84kg).
Propulsion: Rocketdyne Mk 36 Mod 5 single-stage solid motor.
Guidance: Initial optical aiming, IR homing to target heat emitter.
Maximum range: About 5,250 yards (4,800m).
Maximum effective altitude: About 8,200ft (2,500m).
Flight speed: About Mach 2.5.
Warhead: (MIM-72C missile) 28lb (12.7kg) continuous rod HE.

When the purpose-designed Mauler missile was abandoned this weapon was substituted as a makeshift stop-gap, the missile being the original Sidewinder 1C modified for ground launch. A fire unit has four missiles on a manually tracked launcher, carried on an M730 (modified M548) tracked vehicle, with a further eight rounds on board ready to be loaded by hand.

The Chaparral now serves in Air Defence Artillery brigades and is considered a corps asset. Its role is to provide low-level air defense in rear areas. After the fiasco over the purchase of the Roland SAM system, the Chaparral has undergone a modernization programme to allow it to serve into the next century.

worked effectively.

With the success of the Patriot missile in the Gulf War, the fortunes of the air defense arm at last seem to have turned. Now every theater commander wants Patriots to counter the growing threat of ballistic missiles available to many Third World countries.

The Patriot may have grabbed all the headlines during the war with Iraq, but the US Army is not neglecting its existing air defense systems and many programs are underway to improve their performance. Work is also underway to develop an integrated command system known as Forward Area Air Defense Command, Control and Intelligence (FAAD C²I) to co-ordinate divisional air defense weapons.

In 1990, the Hughes Aircraft Company was awarded a procurement contract for the Rosette Scan Seeker guidance seeker section to enhance the missile's aquisition range and infra-red countermeasures rejection capability. A Forward-Looking Infra-Red subsystem has also been added to give the Chaparral an all-weather and night capability. Smokeless motors are also being retrofitted to replace the current "smokey" Rocketdyne Mk 36 Mod 5 single-stage solid powerplant. The M48A1 Chaparral system is typically deployed in composite battalions, 24 units operating alongside 24 M163 Vulcan self-propelled anti-aircraft guns.

Above and left: Chaparral fires four ready rounds (with eight reloads) of MIM-72C missiles. The gunner acquires targets visually or is cued by AN/MPQ-49 forward-area alerting radar, and tracks them optically until the missile's heat-seeking guidance takes over. The US Army has had to make expensive modifications in an attempt to maintain the Chaparral's effectiveness. These have included the retrofitting of launchers with FLIR to permit night and (some) adverse weather operations, and a better guidance system with an enhanced resistance to aircraft infra-red ECM.

Improved Hawk, MIM-23B

Type: Air-defense missile.
Dimensions: Length 16ft 6in (5.03m); body diameter 14in (360mm).; span 48.85in (1,190mm).
Launch weight: 1,383lb (627.3kg).
Propulsion: Aerojet M112 boost/sustain solid rocket motor.
Guidance: CW radar SARH.
Range: 25 miles (40km).
Flight speed: Mach 2.5.
Warhead: HE blast/frag. 165lb (74.8kg).

Hawk (Homing All-the-Way Killer) missiles were first fielded by the US Army in 1960 and were considered very advanced at the time, being the first surface-to-air missile system with continuous wave guidance. It has been exported widely to NATO and Third World countries, and Iran used the missiles to great effect during its war with Iraq after Colonel Oliver North organized the covert delivery of missiles during the infamous Iran-Contra scandal in the mid-1980s.

The HAWK system is intended to provide all-weather air defense at low to medium altitude in the corps and theater rear area, the missiles being deployed in Air Defense Artillery brigades. In spite of a tracked SP carrier, the M727, being available, the system is not very mobile and takes a long time to establish in firing locations. In the 1970s a new version called the Improved HAWK was developed, which featured a larger warhead, improved missile motors and semi-automatic ground systems. Improved HAWK-firing platoons currently comprise a command post, an aquisition radar, a tracking radar, an optical tracker, an Identification Friend or Foe (IFF) system and three or four launchers, each with three missiles. The HAWK missile is guided to its target by reflected radar energy and uses a proximity fuse to detonate its 165lb (74.8kg) HE/fragmentation warhead. In 1989 the US Army began fielding its latest product improvement (PIP III), which provides a low-altitude, simultaneous engagement capability and enhanced electronic countermeasures. The US Army, US Marine Corps and Netherlands are working on improvements to the system's mobility.

It was originally envisaged that the HAWK would be replaced by the Patriot by 1987, but production problems with the new missile led to the

Advanced Anti-Tank Weapon System-Medium (AAWS-M)

Type: Fire-and-forget anti-tank missile.
Weight: Complete system 45lb (20.4kg); missile 32lb (14.5kg).
Guidance: Imaging infra-red seeker, top attack.
Range: 2,187 yards (2,000m).
Warhead: Tandem-shaped charge.

Intended as a replacement for the ageing Dragon as the main infantry platoon anti-tank system. The AAWS-M's fire-and-forget capability will dramatically improve the survivability of the operator. Its infra-red seeker guides the weapon towards tank's thinly-armoured engine decking.

A fixed-price development contract was awarded to Texas Instruments and Martin Marietta, in 1986, and the proof-of-principle flight test programme was completed successfully in 1988. A low-rate production contract was awarded in 1989 and the first field units are scheduled to receive the missiles in 1994.

Above: Three Improved HAWK air-defense missiles are prepared for a test flight from their home-base in Germany.

time-scales slipping to the mid-1990s. The system is still being modernized, so it seems that the HAWK may soldier on for a long time to come. Large numbers of US Army and US Marine Corps HAWKs were deployed to the Middle East during Operations *Desert Sheild/Storm* but saw little service because the coalition air offensive effectively destroyed the Iraqi Air Force on the ground. Some 150 HAWKs were captued from Kuwait by the invading Iraqis in August 1990. A number of coalition pilots reported being illuminated by Iraqi-manned HAWK radars during the Gulf War but no hits were scored.

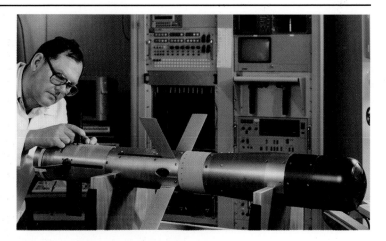

Above: The missile element of the AAWS-M package, seen here in development, weighs in at 32lb (14.5kg).

Patriot, MIM-104

Type: Advanced mobile battlefield SAM system.
Dimensions: Length 209in (5.31m); body diameter 16in (40.6cm); span 36in (92mm).
Launch weight: 2,200lb (998kg).
Propulsion: Thiokol TX-486 single-thrust solid motor.
Guidance: Phased-array radar command and semi-active homing.
Range: About 37 nautical miles (68.6km).
Flight speed: About Mach 3.
Warhead: Choice of nuclear or conventional blast/frag.

After its dramatic Scud missile interceptions during the Gulf War, the Patriot has become one of the US Army's most well-known and popular weapons systems. For many years during the 1980s the Patriot was far from popular in Congress due to its high cost and technical problems associated with bringing the system into service. Production began in 1980 but only got into high gear after 1983, when the first operational units were formed.

The Patriot was originally intended as a theater and tactical high- to medium-altitude anti-aircraft defence system. Currently, the Patriot AIM Capability-Level 2 (PAC-2) missile is in production. To give the system the ability to intercept theatre ballistic missiles, such as the Soviet-made Scud or its Iraqi-made derivatives, Post-Deployment Build-3 (software) modifications were introduced in 1990.

Central to the Patriot system's success is its phased array radar, which allows targets to be detected at several hundred miles range. All tactical functions of the system, airspace surveillance, target detection and tracking and support of missile guidance are controlled by a computerized engagement control system. The combat element of the Patriot system is the fire unit, which consists of a radar set, an engagement control station, a powerplant, antenna mast group and eight remotely located launchers. Each launcher

Right and Below: Test launches of Patriot missiles. The system has been procured by Germany, Japan and The Netherlands as well as the US Army, and plays a major air defence role in NATO.

Above: The phased-array radar system provides surveillance, target tracking and missile guidance facilities. Over 5,000 individual elements form the main antenna, with separate arrays for missile tracking and identification friend-or-foe.

contains four ready-to-fire missiles, each sealed in a container which serves as both shipping container and launch tube.

High-speed digital processing allows the whole Patriot system to be automated, although manual override is possible. Because of the rapid reaction times needed for successful intercepts of ballistic missiles, automatic control is essential in this mode of operation.

To counter the Iraqi Scud threat, 29 Patriot batteries were deployed to defend Saudi Arabia, Israel and Turkey. A total 86 Scud missiles were fired by Iraq during the Gulf War, 47 of which threatened targets defended by Patriots. All these Scuds, apart from two, were successfully intercepted by Patriots, (one Patriot missed and one Patriot failed to launch after a computer failure in the guidance system). The Scud in this last case struck a US barracks in Dhahran, killing 28 soldiers. To increase the effectiveness of the system, engineers from its manufacturer, Raytheon, modified its software during the war to enable the Patriot to intercept the Scud warheads that failed to go ballistic and broke apart on re-entering the earth's atmosphere.

Above: The fire unit is controlled from the Engagement Control Station, although operating procedures are largely automatic.

Above: Before the Gulf War, Patriot had intercepted ballistic missiles such as this Lance in a number of test shots.

Redeye, FIM-43A

Type: Shoulder-fired infantry surface-to-air missile.
Dimensions: Length 48in (122cm); body diameter 2.75in (7cm); span 5.5in (14cm).
Launch weight: 18lb (8.2kg); whole package 29lb (13kg).
Propulsion: Atlantic Research dual-thrust solid.
Guidance: Initial optical aiming, IR homing.
Range: Up to about 2 miles (3.3km).
Flight speed: Mach 2.5.
Warhead: Smooth-case frag.

The first infantry SAM in the world, Redeye entered US Army service in 1964 and some 100,000 have been delivered to the US Army and Marine Corps. It has severe limitations. It has to wait until aircraft have attacked and then fire at their departing tailpipes; there is no IFF. Flight speed is only just enough to catch modern attack aircraft and the guidance is vulnerable to IRCM. Engagement depends on correct identification by the operator of the nature of the target aircraft. He has to wait until the aircraft has passed, aim on a pursuit course, listen for the IR lock-on buzzer, fire the missile, and then select a fresh tube. The seeker cell needs a cooling unit, three of which are packed with each missile tube.

Right: A first-generation man-portable SAM system, Redeye has an operational range of approximately 2 miles (3.3km).

Stinger, FIM-92A

Type: Portable air-defense missile.
Dimensions: (Missile) length 60in (152cm); body diameter 2.75in (7cm); span 5.5in (14cm).
Launch weight: 24lb (10.9kg); whole package 35lb (15.8kg).
Propulsion: Atlantic Research dual-thrust solid.
Guidance: Passive IR homing (see text).
Range: In excess of 3.1 miles (5km).
Flight speed: About Mach 2.
Warhead: Smooth-case frag.

Developed since the mid-1960s as a much-needed replacement for Redeye, Stinger has had a long and troubled development but is at last in service. An improved IR seeker gives all-aspect guidance, the wavelength of less than 4.4 microns being matched to an exhaust plume rather than hot metal, and IFF is incorporated (so that the operator does not have to rely on correct visual identification of oncoming supersonic aircraft).

Stinger made its operational debut with the British SAS during the Falklands War and brought down an Argentine Pucara ground attack aircraft on its first firing at Sana Carlos on 20 May 1982. Subsequently supplied in large numbers to the Afghan *Mujhadeen* guerillas, it was credited with dozens of hits on Soviet Mi-24 Hind helicopter gunships.

The US Army took delivery of its first Stinger in 1982 and they now serve in divisional Air Defence Artillery battalions. Each battalion fields 15 or 20 missile teams which are distributed to brigades and task forces. Most divisions have three battalions. A self-propelled version called the Avenger is entering service; it consists of eight ready-fire missiles mounted on a turret in the rear of an HMMWV.

Right: Whereas Redeye is limited to stern chase. Stinger permits effective attack from all angles, and is more resistant to ECM.

Vulcan, M163/M167

Type: 20mm Vulcan air defence system.
Crew: 1 (on gun).
Weight (firing and traveling): 3,500lb (1,588kg).
Length traveling: 16ft (4.9m).
Width traveling: 6.49ft (1.98m).
Height traveling: 6.68ft (2.03m).
Elevation: −5° to +80°.
Traverse: 360°.
Effective range: 1,750 yards (1,600m).

The 20mm Vulcan is the standard light anti-aircraft gun of the US Army and has been in service since 1968. There are two versions of the Vulcan system in service, one towed and the other self-propelled; both are fair weather, daylight-only systems. The towed version is known as the M167 and this is mounted on a two-wheeled carriage and is normally towed by an M715 or M37 truck. When in the firing position the weapon rests on three outriggers to provide a more stable firing platform. The self-propelled model is known as the M163 and is mounted on a modified M113A1 APC chassis, the chassis itself being the M741.

The 20mm cannon used in the system is a modified version of the air-cooled six-barrel M61 Vulcan cannon developed by General Electric. It is also the standard air-to-air cannon of the US Air Force. The Vulcan cannon has two rates of fire, 1,000 or 3,000 rounds per minute, and the gunner can select either 10, 30, 60 or 100-round bursts. The M163 has 500 rounds of linked ready-use ammunition while the self-propelled model has 1,100 rounds of ready-use ammunition.

The fire control system consists of an M61 gyro lead-computing gun sight, a range-only radar mounted on the right side of the turret (developed by Lockheed Electronics), and a sight current generator. The gunner normally visually acquires and tracks the target while the radar supplies range and range rate data to the sight current generator. These inputs are converted to proper current for use in the sight. With this current the sight computes the correct lead angle and adds the required super elevation.

The turret has full power traverse and elevation, slewing rate being 60°/second, and elevation rate being 45°/second. Power is provided by an auxiliary generator.

The Vulcan air defence system now serves mainly in divisional Air Defence Artillery battalions, with 12 self-propelled fire units equipping each of three ADA battalions in a heavy division. A total of 378 M163s are in service. Light divisions use the M163 in their Air Defence Artillery battalions, which have two or three batteries, each equipped with nine fire units.

Above: The M167A1 is the towed version of Vulcan; this uses linked ammunition whereas SP versions fire linkless rounds.

For many years the Vulcan has been considered inferior to its Soviet counterpart, the ZSU-23-4, but the Sgt. York replacement program ended in disaster during the mid-1980s when costs escalated out of control. Consequently, Vulcan soldiers on.

The 20mm cannon has a maximum effective slant range in the anti-aircraft role of 1,750 yards (1,600m). It can also be used in the ground role, and was deployed to Vietnam for this purpose; in this role it has a maximum range of 4,920 yards (4,500m). A variety of different types of ammunition can be fired, including armor-piercing, armor-piercing incendiary, and high-explosive incendiary. The weapon is also produced for export without the range-only radar. All American M167 VADS now have dual road wheels for improved stability.

Below Left: M163 is the designation for Vulcan mounted on a converted M113 tracked chassis. The Lockheed ranging radar is clearly visible on the side of the turret.

Below: Vulcan is somewhat outclassed by other SP AA systems such as the German Gepard and Soviet ZSU-23-4 and 2S-6. After the failure of the Sergeant York project, however, this elderly equipment will have to serve on for the foreseeable future.

Anti-Tank Weapons

The effectiveness of US Army anti-tank missiles was clearly illustrated early in the Gulf War, when vehicle-and helicopter-mounted TOW missiles devastated Iraqi armoured units during the Battle of Khafji.

Thousands of Hellfire, TOW, Dragon and AT-4 missiles were

Copperhead, M712

Type: Cannon-launched guided projectile (CLGP).
Dimensions: Length 54in (1.37m); diameter 6.1in (115mm).
Launch weight: 140lb (63.5kg).
Propulsion: Fired from gun.
Guidance: Laser homing.
Range: 1.9-10 miles (3-16km).
Flight speed: Supersonic.
Warhead: Shaped charge, 49.6lb (22.5kg).

Conventional artillery, when used in the indirect fire role, has a 1-in-2,500 chance of killing a tank. The US Army started a high-risk program to develop a projectile which could be fired from a standard 155mm weapon (for example, the M109A1 self-propelled gun or the M198 towed howitzer) and hit targets over 7.5 miles (12km) away.

Basic research proved that the project was possible and contracts were awarded to Texas Instruments and Martin Marietta. Each company built a small number of projectiles (termed Cannon-Launched Guided Projectiles) which were tested at the White Sands Missile Range. The Martin Marietta CLGP scored direct hits on both stationary and moving tanks at ranges of 5-7.5 miles (8-12km).

Right: A tripod-mounted version of the AN/TVQ-2 laser locating designator, typical of the Ground Laser Locator Designators that can be used by forward observation teams to "paint" the targets for incoming M712 Copperhead Cannon-Launched Guided Projectiles. The Copperhead will fly down the line of laser energy reflected from the target, impacting on the laser spot.

Below: Having picked up the line of reflected laser energy, the Copperhead can self-correct its trajectory by passing commands to its four control fins. Extremely accurate and highly destructive, the projectile impacts the target (in this case an old M47 tank) at supersonic speed.

used during the war, demonstrating the importance of these hi-tech weapons to the US Army. Only 20 years ago, anti-tank guided weapons were expensive, difficult to operate and highly unreliable. The computer revolution has dramatically reduced their cost and made them very "user-friendly".

The performance of aircraft, helicopter and ground-based laser designators in the Gulf War also validated in a most emphatic way the effectiveness of remote weapon guidance concepts and the US Army looks set to invest heavily in this area of technology during the 1990s.

The projectile hit the target despite deliberate aiming errors of several hundred meters. In September 1975 a CLGP hit a stationary M48 tank 5 miles (8km) away while the target was being illuminated by a laser carried in a Prairie IIA RPV. The RPV located the target with a TV camera, focusing on the target, and signalled the artillery to fire a CLGP. As a result of these trials, Martin Marietta was awarded a contract for full-scale development of the CLGP.

The basic idea is that a forward observer sees an enemy tank approaching. He then radios its approximate position to the artillery and one weapon fires a CLGP in the general direction of the target. Once the CLGP is on its way the forward observer illuminates the target with his Ground Laser Locator Designator (or GLLD), the CLGP senses the reflected laser energy and, by applying

commands to its control fins, flies into the laser spot on the target. It can be steered into the target provided the nomal gun-aiming point is within about 0.7 miles (1.1km) of it. Copperhead is treated like any other gun ammunition.

Throughout its development program, the Copperhead was dogged by escalating costs, and in the first seven years of the program the unit price escalated from $5,500 per round to $37,632. By the mid-1980s, the problems with the weapon had been resolved and some 30,000 Copperheads were subsequently purchased.

The US Army's faith in the system was rewarded during the Gulf War, when III Corps and VIII Corps artillery fired 90 Copperhead rounds against hardened Iraqi targets, achieving "a high success rate". Laser designation/terminal guidance was carried out by forward artillery observer teams and OH-58D helicopters.

Dragon, M47, FGM-77A

Type: Infantry anti-tank/assault missile.
Dimensions: Length 29.3in (74cm); body diameter 4.5in (11.4cm); fin span 13in (33cm).
Launch weight: 24.4lb (11.1kg).
Propulsion: Recoilless gas-generator thruster in launch tube; sustain propulsion by 60 small side thrusters fired in pairs upon tracker demand.
Guidance: See text.
Range: 200 to 3,300ft (60-1,000m).
Flight speed: About 230mph (370km/h).
Warhead: Linear shaped charge, 5.4lb (2.45kg).

Dragon was designed as a medium-range complement to TOW (*qv*). In service since 1971, Dragon comes sealed in a glass-fiber launch tube with a fat rear end containing the launch charge. The operator attaches this to his tracker comprising telescopic sight, IR sensor and electronics box. When the missile is fired its three curved fins flick open and start the missile spinning. The operator holds the sight on the target and the tracker automaticaly commands the missile to the line of sight by firing appropriate pairs of side thrusters. The launch tube is thrown away and a fresh one attached to the tracker.

   The Dragon system is not without its problems. Perhaps the most important is that the missile body diameter of 4.5in (11.4cm) sets the limit on the size of the warhead. The effectiveness of a shaped charge warhead is a function of its diameter, and at least 6in (15cm) is likely to be needed to counter the new armors coming into service on the latest Soviet tanks. In addition, the missile is slow; this aggravates the difficulties of the operator, who must hold his breath throughout the flight of the missile. The operator is also adjured to grasp the launch-tube tightly, for if he does not his shoulder may rise at the moment of launch, thus sending the missile into the ground. Finally, the rocket thrusters have been found to deteriorate in storage, and many need early replacement.

   The Dragon saw service during the invasion of Grenada, Operation *Just Cause* and during the Gulf War. While it proved effective in these operations, especially when employed against enemy infantry bunkers, the US Army recognises that its warhead is insufficient to deal with the latest Soviet main battle tank armor.

Below: Dragon is a lightweight, portable missile which gives infantry platoons a reasonable anti-armor capability.

Above: Once the missile is fired from its launch tube it is steered by pulses from small thrusters around the missile body.

Below: A thermal imaging system can be attached to the sight unit for night and poor weather operations.

Hellfire, AGM-114

Type: Laser-guided anti-tank missile.
Dimensions: Length 64in (1.626m); body diameter 7in (0.178m).
Launch weight: 98.86lb (44.84kg).
Propulsion: Thiokol TX657 reduced smoke "all-boost" motors.
Guidance. Laser homing.
Range: 5 miles (8km).
Flight speed: Builds to Mach 1.17.
Warheads: 9kg multi-purpose shaped charge, anti-armor shaped charge, flechette, smoke, illumination, anti-radar chaff.

Considered to be the most advanced anti-tank missile in the US Army's inventory, Hellfire uses third-generation technology to guide itself to a target designated by laser. Ground or aircraft laser designators are compatible with the missile. The Hellfire can be used in a variety of modes: autonomous, air or ground, direct or indirect, single shot, rapid or ripple fire. Its guidance system can achieve target lock after launch and respond to designation from multiple sources. Currently, the missile is the main weapons system of the AH-64A Apache attack helicopter.

Four versions are in service or under development. The basic Hellfire has been in production since 1983, with some 35,000 in service. Improved Hellfire has a precursor designed to penetrate reactive armor. The Hellfire Optimised Missile System (HOMS) is planned to enter service in 1993-96 and features improved penetration of HOMS with a millimeter-wave seeker for use with the new LONGBOW Apache helicopter's millimeter-wave radar. It will be a true "fire-and-forget" missile, requiring no guidance or laser designation during flight.

More than 2,900 Hellfires were fired by US Army Apaches and Kiowa Warriors, and US Marine Corps AH-1W Cobra attack helicopters during the Gulf War. Outstanding accuracy was recorded.

Above right: Groundcrewmen raise a Hellfire AGM onto the four-point pylon beneath an Apache's port wing. Note the guidance fins.

Right: The Apache/Hellfire team proved its fighting prowess in most spectacular fashion from the outset of the Gulf War.

Lightweight Multi-Purpose Weapon (AT-4)

Type: Single shot, throwaway, squad anti-tank rocket.
Caliber: 84mm.
Dimensions: Length 39.7in (1.008m).
Launch weight: Complete unit 14.6lb (6,62kg).
Guidance: Iron sights.
Range: 328+ yards (300+m).
Muzzle Velocity: 951.4ft/s (290m/s).
Warhead: Fin-stabilized, HE-shaped.

The AT-4 is currently in production to supplement the ubiquitous M72A1, as the US Army's infantry squad anti-armor/close support weapon. The M72A1 LAW is now getting very old and is not considered capable of defeating the latest Soviet tank armor.

First deliveries began in 1989, direct from FFV of Sweden, but Alisant Techsystems Inc, Minnetonkia, MN, has now begun licensed production at the Joliet Army Ammunition Plant in Illinois.

Above: A shoulder-fired recoilless weapon, the AT-4 LAW will be used against soft-skinned and lightly-armored targets.

TOW, BGM-71

Type: Heavy anti-tank missile.
Propulsion: Hercules K41 boost (0.05s) and sustain (1s) motors.
Dimensions: Length 45 to 75in (1,162mm); body diameter 6in (152mm); span (wings extended) 13.5in (343mm).
Launch weight: (BGM-71A) 46.1lb (20.9kg).
Range: 1,640 to 12,300ft (500 to 3,750m).
Flight speed: 625mph (1,003km/h).
Warhead: (BGM-71A) Picatinny Arsenal 8.6lb (3.9kg) shaped charge with 5.3lb (2.4kg) explosive.

The TOW (Tube-launched, Optically-tracked, Wire-guided) missile is likely to set an all-time record in the field of guided-missile production. Prime contractor Hughes Aircraft began work in 1965 to replace the 106mm recoilless rifle. The missile's basic infantry form is supplied in a sealed tube which is clipped to the launcher. The missile tube is attached to the rear of the launch tube, the target sighted and the round fired. The boost charge pops the missile from the tube, firing through lateral nozzles amidships. The four wings indexed at 45° spring open forwards, and the

Below: Spectacular backblast erupts as TOW streaks from its launch tube. If an alert enemy spots this, he may have a few seconds to take countermeasures such as firing defensive smoke.

four tail controls flip open rearwards. Guidance commands are generated by the optical sensor in the sight, which continuously measures the position of a light source in the missile relative to the LOS and sends steering commands along twin wires. These drive the helium-pressure actuators working the four tail controls in pairs for pitch and yaw.

Early-model TOW's made their combat debut in the early-1970s and also saw large scale service during the 1973 Arab-Israeli War. Most US Army units now field TOW missiles on a variety of platforms, including AH-1 Cobra attack helicopters, Bradley fighting vehicles, Improved TOW vehicles and HUM-VEEs. Infantry units use a man-portable version with a tripod mount. The TOW missile has been produced in larger numbers than any other US missile and has been exported widely.

An aggressive program is underway to improve the missile and ensure its effectiveness against the latest Soviet reactive tank armor into the next century. The TOW-2 missile has been in production at Hughes Aircraft Company's Tuscon plant since the early-1980s. It features a 21.25in (540mm) probe that is intended to detonate reactive armor and allow the main warhead to penetrate its target's conventional armor.

Older, basic TOW and Improved TOW launchers have been upgraded to TOW-2 standard. Thermal night sights are now standard on all TOW launchers and a sight improvement program is underway. The US Army continues to purchase around 10,000 TOW-2s a year, and since November 1990 the TOW-2B, which features improved penetration capability, has been in production. Numerous tank kills were recorded by the missile during the Gulf War, including many top-of-the-line Soviet T-72s.

Small Arms

Over the past 30 years the US Army's small arms programs have been some of its most controversial, causing rifts with allies over ammunition standardization, disputes with Congress about the selection of contractors, and generating terrible publicity over the relability of the M16.

M16A1/A2

Type: Rifle.
Caliber: 5.56mm.
Length overall (with flash suppressor). 38.9in (99cm).
Length of barrel: 36.4in (92.4cm).
Weight (including 30-round loaded magazine): 8.9lb (4.03kg).
Range (maximum effective): 300 yards (274m).
Rate of fire: 700-900rpm (cyclic).
Muzzle velocity: M198 (ball) 3,251ft/s (991m/s), (SS109) 3,110ft/s (948.5m/s).

The M16 (previously the AR-15) was designed by Eugene Stoner and was a development of the earlier 7.62mm AR-10 assault rifle. It was first adopted by the US Air Force, and at a later date the US Army adopted the weapon for use in Vietnam. When first used in combat numerous faults became apparent, and most of these were traced to a lack of training and poor maintenance. Since then the M16 has replaced the 7.62mm M14 as the standard rifle of the United States forces. To date over 5,000,000 have been manufactured, most by Colt Firearms and the weapon was also made under licence in Singapore, South Korea and the Philippines. Twenty-one armies use the M16. The weapon is gas-operated and the user can select either full automatic or semi-automatic. Both 20- and 30-round magazines can be fitted, as can a bipod, bayonet, telescope and night sight. The weapon can also be fitted with the M203 40mm grenade launcher, and this fires a variety of 40mm grenades to a maximum range of 382 yards (350m). The M203 has now replaced the M79 grenade launcher on a one-for-one

In recent years, the US Army and Congress seems to have got the issue into proportion and some sensible decisions have been made over the replacement of the M1911A1 0.45in pistol and adoption of the NATO 5.56mm round as the standard small arms ammunition.

Shrinking defense budgets mean that US small arms programs are becoming tri-service in composition, and the Pentagon now has to take into account the needs of all services during the development of new weapons. The Mk 19-3, for example, is a key weapon for USAF security police.

---

basis. The Colt Commando is a special version of the M16 and this has a shorter barrel, flash suppresor and a telescopic sight, reducing the overall length of the weapon to 27.9in (71cm). The M231 is a special model which can be fired from within the M2 Bradley Infantry Fighting Vehicle.

There has been consistent dissatisfaction with the M16A1 in the US Army, and even more so in the other main user — the US Marine Corps. One of the major complaints is its lack of effectiveness at ranges above 340 yards (300m), which has come to a head with the increased emphasis on desert warfare with the RDF. This, combined with the high average age of current stocks, led to a major review in 1981.

The latest version of the weapon, the M16A2, has been in full-scale production since 1987 under a five-year fixed-price contract with FN Manufacturing Inc. Some 270,000 weapons are in service and conversion kits are also being produced to allow old-model M16A1s to be converted to the new standard.

Incorporated in the new weapon are an improved rear sight, pistol grip and stock. Accuracy is improved by virtue of a new muzzle compensator, three-round burst control and a heavier barrel. The main change is in the weapon's rifling which allows the NATO standard 5.56mm ammuniton round to be used.

Below: Lying low, a soldier takes careful aim at a target with his M16A1. Synonymous with the US Army soldier for some three decades, this rifle has nevertheless had a checkered service life, primarily because of its diminished accuracy at ranges in excess of 340 yards (300m). The improved M16A2 can be fired in semi-automatic mode and with a three-round burst.

M9 9mm Personal Defense Weapon

Type: Pistol.
Caliber: 9mm.
Length: 8.6in (217m).
Length of barrel: 4.92in. (125mm).
Weight Loaded: 2.6lbs (1.17kg).
Effective range: 54.6 yards (50m).
Muzzle Velocity: 1,279.5ft/s (390m/s).

The M1911 0.45in (11.4mm) pistol served as the standard US military side arm from World War One onwards. The weapon's performance was legendary and there was little incentive for the Pentagon to consider replacing it. By the 1980s, however, the famous "45" was becoming evermore expensive to maintain in service and NATO had adopted the 9mm round as its standard pistol ammunition. A shoot-off in 1982 failed to produce an outright winner, but the Pentagon kept pressing the case for a new weapon. In 1985 it awarded a five-year, fixed-price contract to Beretta USA to produce 315,930 examples of its 92SB pistol, under the US military designation M9 9mm Personal Defense Weapon. A follow-on contract with options for 500,000 weapons was signed in 1989.

The pistol is semi-automatic and double-action. It uses a 15-round magazine, fitted in the pistol grip. NATO standard 9mm ammunition is fired. Overall, the weapon is lighter than the old "45" and can be used by either left- or right-handed shooters. The weapon is issued to personnel who are not classed as riflemen for personal defence, such as law-enforcement servicemen, senior officers and aviators. To date, more than 150,000 M9s

M60

Type: General-purpose machine-gun.
Caliber: 7.62mm.
Length: 43.3in (110cm).
Length of barrel: 22in (56cm).
Weight: 23lb (10.48kg) with bipod; 39.6lb (18kg) with tripod.
Maximum effective range (bipod): 984 yards (900m).
Maximum effective range (tripod): 1,968 yards (1,800m).
Rate of fire: 550rpm (cyclic); 200rpm (automatic).

This weapon was developed by the Bridge Tool and Die Works and the Inland Division of General Motors Corporation, under the direction of the Springfield Armory. Production of the M60 was initiated in 1959 by the Maremont Corporation of Saco, Maine.

The M60 is gas-operated, air-cooled and is normally used with a 100-round belt of ammunition. To avoid overheating the barrel is normally changed after 500 rounds have been fired. Its fore sight is of the fixed blade type and its rear sight is of the U-notch type and is graduated from some 656ft to 3,937ft (200 to 1200m) in about 328ft (100m) steps. The weapon is provided with a stock, carrying handle and a built in bipod. The M60

Right: An M60 bursts into life in support of ground forces operating as part of Operation *Desert Storm*. This particular example is attached to an M4 pedestal mount, one of several mount options available for the land-based version of this classic GPMG. The gunner's colleague is feeding through the belted ammunition, which comes in 100-round clips. Maximum rate of fire is 550rpm.

Above: A semi-automatic double-action pistol that is lighter, safer and more lethal than the venerable M1911 0.45in pistol, the M9 9mm Personal Defense Weapon can be used effectively by both left- and right-handed shooters.

have been delivered to all four US services, but budget cuts are taking their toll on the programme and all services are cutting back purchases. So the M1911 will live on!

---

can also be used on an M122 tripod mount, M4 pedestal mount and M142 gun mount for vehicles. Other versions include the M60C remote for helicopters, M60D pintle mount for vehicles and helicopters and the M60E2 internal model for AFVs.

The M60 provides US infantry units with immense firepower and it will remain in service for many years. No immediate successor is being considered by the US Army at present.

M2 HB

Type: Heavy machine-gun.
Caliber: 0.50in (12.7mm).
Length overall: 65.07in (165.3cm).
Length of barrel: 44.99in (114.3cm).
Weight (gun only): 83.33lb (37.8kg); 127.8lb (57.98kg) with tripod.
Range: 1,996 yards (1,825m) effective in ground role; 7,470 yards (6,830m) maximum; 820 yards (750m) anti-aircraft role.

The 0.50in caliber M2 machine-gun was developed for the US Army in the early-1930s, as a replacement for the 0.50in M1921A1 MG. The weapon was developed by John Browning (who designed many other famous weapons including the Browning Automatic Rifle and the Browning 0.30in machine-gun), and the Colt Firearms company of Hartford, Connecticut.

The M2 is air-cooled and recoil operated, and is fed from a disintergrating metallic link belt. The weapon can fire either single shot or full automatic, and various types of ammunition can be fired including ball, tracer, armor-piercing and armor-piercing incendiary. For ground targets the weapon is mounted on the M3 tripod while for the anti-aircraft role the M63 mount is used. It is also mounted on many armored fighting vehicles including the M113A1 series of APC (and variants), the M109/M108 SPH and the M578 and M88 ARV. The US Army stopped purchasing the M2 HB just after World War Two, but its inventory is periodically rebuilt to keep it operational. On a number of occasions the production line has been re-opened to supply export customers. "HB" in the designation stands for "hydraulic buffer", a modification introduced in the late-1930s.

M72A2

Type: Light Anti-Tank Weapon (LAW).
Caliber: 66mm.
Length of rocket: 20in (50.8cm).
Weight of rocket: 2.2lb (1kg).
Muzzle velocity: 476ft/s (145m/s).
Maximum effectve range: 355 yards (325m).
Length of launcher closed: 25.7in (65.5cm).
Length of launcher extended: 35in (89.3cm).
Weight complete: 4.75lb (2.15kg).

The M72 is the standard Light Anti-Tank Weapon (LAW) of the US Army and is also used by many other armies around the world. Development of weapon started in 1958 with the first production LAWs being completed by the Hesse Eastern Company of Brockton, Massachusetts, in 1962. It is also manufactured under licence in Norway by Raufoss. The LAW is a lightweight, shoulder-fired rocket launcher and its rocket has a HEAT warhead which will penetrate over 11.8in (300mm) of armor.

When the M72 is required for action, the infantryman removes the safety pins, which open the end covers, and the inner tube is telescoped outwards, cocking the firing mechanism. The launcher tube is then held over the shoulder, aimed and the weapon fired. The launcher is then discarded. Improved models are known as the M72A1 and the more recent M72A2.

The M72 has been used extensively in combat by the US Army and other armies. While its effectiveness against tanks has been reduced by advances in armor technology, such as Chobham and reactive armor, the M72 still provides a key part of the infantry squad's close-quarters firepower. British forces found it very useful in dealing with Argentine bunkers during the Falklands War, and 82nd Airborne Division paratroopers used

Above: The M2 HB on an M3 tripod. It is fed from a 100-round disintegrating-link belt at a cyclic rate of fire of 450-575 rounds per minute. The history of this weapon can be traced back to 1933, when the 0.50in M1921 machine-gun was renamed the M2 HV (Heavy Barrel). That it continues to be used by the US Army nearly 60 years after its debut, albeit in smaller quantities and after several terminations of production, is a fitting testimony to its sturdy design and excellent fighting qualitities.

Above: The effective range of the M72A2 LAW against a range of stationary "soft" targets is in the region of 355 yards (325m), but less than half that distance when fired against moving targets. This lightweight, compact weapon is giving way to the AT-4 Lightweight Multipurpose Weapon, which is more accurate and lethal, and which has greater range.

the M72 extensively in Grenada, Panama and the Gulf War. The US Army has had great difficulty fielding a replacement and ended up buying the AT-4 off-the-shelf from Sweden.

Mk19-3

Type: Automatic grenade launcher.
Caliber: 40mm.
Length: 40.4in (1.028m).
Weight: 72.5lb (32.88kg).
Range: 1,640 yards (1,500m) (point targets); 2,405 yards (2,200m) (area targets).
Rate-of-fire: 325-375 rounds per minute.
Muzzle Velocity: 787.4ft/sec (240/sec).

Curiously, this highly-effective weapon system started life as a program for the US Navy in 1981. The first Mk19-3s entered US Army service in 1983 with the 9th Infantry Division. In 1988, the US Army took over the program and awarded a multi-year contract to the SACO Defence Company Inc. for large-scale production.

The Mk19-3 provides close-range firepower against personnel and light armor for light forces, and units engaged in rear area security, such as military police units. A tripod mount enables the weapon to be man-portable. Other mounts have been developed to fit the Mk19-3 to M113 APCs, HUM-VEEs, trucks and M88A1 recovery vehicles.

Against personnel in the open, the MK19-3 has an expected casualty radius of 16.5ft (5m), and in the anti-armor role it can penetrate two inches (5cm) of armor at up to 2,405 yards (2,200m) range.

Below: Originally developed on behalf of the US Navy, the 40mm Mk19-3 automatic grenade launcher was embraced by the US Army in the second half of the 1980s. Its formidable firepower is backed up by its operational versatility, thanks to a series of mounts which allow it to be fired from a variety of trucks and APC's now in US Army service. The large magazine unit visible on the port side of the gun can hold up to 50 grenades.

M79

Type: Grenade launcher.
Caliber: 40mm.
Weight of grenade: 0.610lb (0.277kg).
Length of launcher: 29in (73.7cm).
Length of barrel: 14in (35.6cm).
Weight of launcher: (empty) 5.99lb (2.72kg); loaded 6.5lb (2.95kg).
Muzzle velocity: 249ft/s (76m/s).
Range: 437.4 yards (400m) maximum; 383 yards (350m) effective, area targets; 164 yards (150m) effective, point targets.
Effective casualty radius: 5.46 yards (5m).
Rate of fire: 5 rounds per minute.

The 40mm M79 Grenade Launcher was developed to give the infantryman the capability to deliver accurate firepower to a greater range than could be achieved with a conventional rifle grenade. The M79 is a single shot, break-open weapon and is fired from the shoulder. It is breech loaded and fires a variety of different types of ammunition including high explosive, high explosive air burst, VCS gas and smoke. Its fore sight is of the blade type and its rear sight is of the folding leaf adjustable type. The latter is graduated from 82 yards (75m) to 410 yards (375m) in about 27 yards (25m) increments. When the rear sight is in the horizontal position, the fixed sight may be used to engage targets up to 109.3 yards (100m). The M79 has been replaced in front line units by the M203 grenade launcher which is fitted to the standard M16A1 rifle.

M249

Type: Squad automatic weapon (SAW).
Caliber: 5.56mm.
Lengths: Overall 39.4in (100cm); barrel 18.5in (47cm).
Weights: Empty 15.5lb (7.03kg); with 200-round magazine 22lb (9.97kg).
Effective range: 1,421 yards (1,300m).
Rate of fire: 750rpm.
Muzzle velocity: 3,033ft/s (924m/s).

The SAW idea was conceived in 1966, but it has taken a long time to reach service. When the M16 was issued to infantry squads, all infantrymen had an automatic weapon, but with a maximum effective range of some 330 yards (300m) only. It was considered that each fire team in the squad needed a weapon of greater all-round capability than the M16, but obviously not a weapon as heavy or as sophisticated as the M60. The SAW meets this requirement, and has been issued on a scale of one per fire team, ie, two per squad. The SAW may also replace some M60s in non-infantry units.

The M249 SAW is a development of the Belgian Fabrique Nationale (FN) "Minimi". FN Manufacturing, Inc. began producing the M249 in South Carolina in 1984 under a five-year contract. The weapon is issued on a scale of two M249s per US Army infantry squad and three per US Marine Corps infantry squad.

The M249 is very smooth in operation and displays a realiability that is considered exceptional in light machine guns. Fully combat ready, with a magazine of 200 rounds, bipod, sling, and cleaning kit, the M249 weighs 22lb (9.97kg), which is still 1lb (0.4kg) less than an empty M60 machine gun. The M855 ball round fired from the M249 will penetrate a US steel helmet at a range of 1,421 yards (1,300m).

Overall, the M249 is superior to the Soviet PKM 7.62mm (bigger, heavier, smaller mag), and the RPK 5.45mm (bigger, lighter, smaller mag).

Above: Largely replaced in service by the M203/M16A1 rifle combination, the M79 fires the full range of 40mm grenades.

Above: The M249, which is better than the M16, especially at extended ranges. It is left-hand fed from a 200-round container.

Vehicles

"Amateurs talk tactics, professionals talk logistics" is a common phrase in the US Army and reflects its attitude to keeping combat units supplied with ammunition, food and other essential supplies. In many armies support vehicles receive little attention or interest, but the US Army realises their importance and invests heavily in them.

HMMWV

Type: High mobility, multi-purpose wheeled vehicle (HMMWV).
Dimensions: Length 15ft (4.57m); width 7ft (2.15m); height 5ft 9in (1.75m).
Weights: Empty 4,969lb (2,254kg); maximum 8,532lb (3,870kg).
Engine: General Motors V-8, 6.2l diesel, 130hp at 3,600rpm.
Performance: Maximum road speed 65mph (105km/h); road range 351 miles (565km); gradient 60 per cent

The HMMWV is now to be found in almost every unit and branch of the US Army, carrying out an amazing variety of tasks. Originally called the Hummer by its manufacturers, the name never caught on with US servicemen who preferred the term HUM-VEE, derived from its US Army designation — High Mobility, Multi-purpose Wheeled Vehicle (HMMWV). Since the first versions came off LTV's production line in Mishawaka in 1981, the basic M998 HUM-VEE has been modified to fulfill many different requirements by all four US services. In 1991 the US Army paid $38,638 a piece for a basic HUM-VEE.

Three ambulance versions have been produced: the M996, M997 and M1035. There are two command post shelter versions: the M1037 and

The US Army maintains a massive vehicle fleet, containing every imagineable type from simple trucks to ambulances, specialist engineering and ammunition-carrying vehicles to armored bridge-layers.

For many years the most famous US Army vehicle was the World War Two-vintage Willys Jeep, but since the Gulf War its modern equillent — the HMMWV, or HUM-VEE as it is called by US servicemen — has taken center stage. The US Army's initial purchase of 40,000 HUM-VEEs was such a success that a follow-on batch of 33,000 was ordered in 1989.

M1042. For reconnaissance and rear area security missions four armored HUM-VEEs have been produced: the M1043, M1025, M1026 and M1044. An armored TOW anti-tank version is designated the M1045, and unarmored TOW versions are the M966, M1036 and M1046. A specialist gun tractor for the M119 light gun is the M1069, which can carry a six-man crew and 22 rounds of ammunition.

At first the HUM-VEE had a notorious reputation for unreliability, but it turned in an outstanding performance during the Gulf War, earning itself an enviable reputation as a "go anywhere, do anything" military vehicle.

In late-1991, the financially-troubled LTV Corporation agreed to sell AM General Corporation, maker of the HUM-VEE, to the Renco Corporation of New York. The Indiana-based AM General Corporation has produced 95,000 HUM-VEEs to date, the vast majority of which have gone to the US Army. Over 6,000 examples have already been supplied to overseas customers, with further export orders outstanding from no less than 21 nations.

Below: A pair of HMMWVs plough their way back through the desert sands of Saudi Arabia, at the end of a reconnaissance patrol as part of Operation Desert Storm. This modern-day successor to the ubiquitous Jeep has proved its versatility time and time again, winning many friends within the US Army in the process.

M60 (AVLB)

Type: Armored vehicle-launched bridge.
Crew: 2 (commander; driver).
Armament: None.
Armor: Front 4in-4·72in (101-120mm); sides 2in (51mm).
Dimensions (vehicle): Length 28ft 4in (8·648m); width 12ft (3·657m); height 10ft 4in (3·162m).
Weight (vehicle): 91,900lb (41,685kg).
Engine: Continental AVDS-1790-2A, 12-cylinder diesel; 750bhp at 2,400rpm.
Performance: Road speed 30mph (48·28km/h); range 310 miles (500km); fording 4ft (1·22m); gradient 60 per cent; vertical obstacle 3ft (0·91m); trench 8ft 6in (2·59m).

The US Army's requirement for a tactical bridge is met by the M60 AVLB, although numbers of M48 AVLBs remain in service. So far as is known, there are no current plans to develop an AVLB version of the M1.

The M60 AVLB can use a variety of bridges. The first weighs 31,900lb (14,470kg) and is made of aluminum. It is 63ft (19·2m) long and can span a gap of 60ft (18·3m), taking 3 minutes to launch and from 10 to 60 minutes to recover (depending on the ground). The second bridge weighs 19,000lb (8,618kg), has an overall length of 92ft 10in (28·3m), and can span 88ft 7in (27m). Both have a Bridge Classification of Type 60; ie, they will take a load of 60 tons.

Other types of bridging used by the US Army include the Mobile Assault Bridge/Ferry (MAB) and the British-designed Medium Girder Bridge (MGB).

Below: The highly mobile M60 chassis without turret, fitted with a hydraulic cylinder assembly and a scissors bridge.

Above: An M113 mounted with Vulcan air defense system trundles across an AVLB emplaced by the M60 chassis parked on the bank.

M88A1

Type: Medium armored recovery vehicle.
Crew: 4 (commander, driver, co-driver, mechanic).
Armament: One 0.50 M2 HB machine-gun.
Dimensions: Length (without dozer blade): 27.15ft (8.267m); width 11.24ft (3.428m); height (with anti-aircraft machine-gun) 10.58ft (3.225m).
Weight: 111,993lb (50,800kg).
Ground pressure: 1.63lb/in² (0.74kg/cm²).
Engine: Continental AVSI-1790-2DR diesel engine developing 750bhp at 2,400rpm.
Performance: Road speed 26mph (42km/hr); range 280 miles (450km); vertical obstacle 3.49ft (1.066m); trench 8.58ft (2.6m); gradient 60 per cent.

The standard medium armored recovery vehicle used by the US Army in the early-1950s was the M74. This was based on a Sherman tank chassis but could not handle the heavier tanks which were then entering service. In 1954, work on a new medium armored recovery vehicle commenced and three prototypes, designated the T88, were built by Bowen-McLaughlin-York. After trials, a batch of pre-production vehicles was built and then Bowen-McLaughlin-York were awarded a production contract for the vehicle which was standardized as the M88. Just over 1,000 M88s were built between 1961 and 1964, and some were also exported abroad. The M88 uses many automotive components of the M48 tank, and can recover AFVs up to and including the M60 MBT. Its role on the battlefield is to recover damaged and disabled tanks and other AFVs, and it can, if required, remove major components from tanks such as complete turrets. When the M88 first entered service it was armed with a 0.50in caliber machine-gun mounted in a turret, but this was subsequently replaced by a simple pintle mounted 0.50in machine-gun.

The hull of the M88 is of cast armor construction and provides the crew with protection from small arms fire and shell splinters. The crew compartment is at the front of the hull and the engine and transmission are at the rear. A hydraulically operated dozer blade is mounted at the

Below: As in most armies, the crew of the bogged down or broken vehicle (in this case an M60 requiring an engine change) are expected to carry out the heavy preparation work while the M88 recovery crew await the chance to use their specialist skills.

Above: The M88A1 is used to recover virtually every type of AFV now in US Army service, although its undoubted abilities do not extend to recovery of the M1A1 Abrams. This shortfall may be rectified in the future by virtue of the M88A1E.

front of the hull and this is used to stabilize the vehicle when the winch or "A" frame is being used, and can also be used for normal dozing operations. The "A" type frame is pivoted at the front of the hull, and when not required this lies in the horizontal position on top of the hull. This frame can lift a maximum load of six tons (5,443kg), or 25 tons (22,680kg) with the dozer blade in the lowered position.

The M88 is provided with two winches and both of these are mounted under the crew compartment. The main winch is provided with 200ft (61m) of 32mm cable and has a maximum pull of 40 tons, whilst the secondary winch, which is used for hoisting operations, has 200ft (61m) of 16mm cable. The vehicle is provided with a full range of tools and an auxiliary fuel pump. This enables the vehicle to transfer fuel to other armored vehicles.

By February 1982, the US Army had completed the conversion of its M88 fleet into M88A1s. This improved version boasted a 750bph AVDS-1790-2DR diesel engine. Deliveries of the factory-new M88A1s continued until 1989. Some 2,500 are currently in the US Army inventory. In 1990 six prototypes of a new version, the M88A1E1, were built to allow for the recovery of the M1A1 in all tactical situations, but the US Army has not yet decided whether to progress with the program.

M578

Type: Light armored recovery vehicle.
Crew: 3.
Armament: One 0.50in M2 HB machine-gun.
Dimensions: Length overall 21ft (6.42m); width 10.331ft (3.149m); height with machine-gun 11.20ft (3.416m).
Weight: 53,572lb (24,300kg).
Ground pressure: 1.56lb/in² (0.71kg/cm²).
Engine: General Motors Model 8V71T eight cylinder liquid diesel developing 425bhp at 2,300rpm.
Performance: Road speed 34mph (54.71km/h); range 450 miles (725km); vertical obstacle 3.3ft (1.016m); trench 7.76ft (2.362m); gradient 60 per cent.

During the 1950's the Pacific Car and Foundry Company of Renton, Washington, was awarded a contract by the US Army to build a new range of self-propelled artillery, all of which were to use the same common chassis. These three weapons were the T235 (which eventually entered service as the 175mm M107), the T236 (which entered service as the 8in M110) and the T245 (this was a 155mm weapon but was not developed past the prototype stage). In 1957, it was decided to build a range of light armored recovery vehicles using the same chassis as the self-propelled guns. Three different prototypes were built. Further development resulted in the T120E1 and this entered service as the M578.

The first production M578 was completed by the FMC Corporation in 1962, and since then the vehicle has been produced by the designers, Pacific Car and Foundry, and more recently by Bowen-McLaughlin-York.

With the replacement of the M113 by the Bradley and improvements that have boosted the weight of the M109, the M578 is fast becoming obsolete because it cannot pull these heavy vehicles. Consequently, the US Army is slowly retiring its M578s.

Apart from recovering such vehicles as the M110 and M109, the vehicle is also used to change major components in the field, such as engines, transmissions, and tank barrels.

The hull of the M578 is identical to that of the M107 and M110 self-propelled guns, with the driver being seated at the front of the hull on the left side and the engine to his right. The crane is mounted at the rear of the hull and this can be traversed through a full 360 degrees. The commander and mechanic are seated in the turret and a standard 0.50 Browning M2 HB machine-gun is mounted on the roof for anti-aircraft protection. The crane can lift a maximum of 13.38 tons (13,600kg) and the main winch is provided with 229ft (70m) of 25mm cable. This has a maximum capacity of 26.57 tons (27,000kg). A large spade is mounted at the rear of the hull to stabilize the vehicle when the winch or crane is being used; in addition, the suspension can be locked out if required. Unlike most MBTs, the M578 is not provided with an NBC system and it has no amphibious capability. Infra-red driving lights are normally fitted. Unlike many other combat support vehicles in service with the US Army, the basic M578 has not spawned any derivatives.

Above: The M578 is designed to recover vehicles up to 66,137lb (30,000kg), and therefore could recover the Army's SPGs and APCs (and engines, gun barrels and so on), but not main battle tanks (the M1 weighs 149,950lb/68,075kg). The two-winch capacity is 60,000lb (27,216kg) bare drum, and hoisting capacity is 15,000lb (6,804kg). Besides the driver there are a commander and a mechanic, who normally enter the turret through side doors, although there are also double doors at the rear. They each have a single-piece hatch cover and six periscopes. A machine-gun mounted in front of the left hatch cover is provided for use against attacking aircraft. The M578 uses the M110 chassis; there are no variants in service.

M992 FAASV

Type: Field artillery ammunition support vehicle (FAASV).
Crew: 9 (maximum).
Armament: One 0.50in Browning MG.
Dimensions: Length overall 22ft 3in (6.7m); width 10ft 10in (3.295m); height 10ft 7½in (3.24m).
Weights: Loaded 57,500lb (26,082kg); cargo capacity 18,920lb (8,582kg).
Engine: Detroit Diesel Model 8V71T, 8-cylinder turbocharged diesel; 405bhp at 2,350rpm.
Performance: Road speed 35mph (56km/h); road range 220 miles (354km); vertical obstacle 1ft 9in (0.53m); trench 6ft (1.83).

Many armies are searching for an answer to the ammunition resupply problem created by the ever-increasing capability of modern artillery. This problem has a number of facets. First, most artillery is now on highly mobile self-propelled tracked chassis, and is thus able to move more often, faster, and to more inaccessible sites. Secondly, rates of fire are increasing and thus creating a greater quantitative requirement. Finally, .increases in

Inset: The M992 has supported M109 and M110 batallions in Europe since the mid-1980s. The rear door provides overhead protection.

Below: Capable of carrying 48 x 8in (203mm) rounds for the M110A2 SP howitzer, the highly-mobile FAASV speeds up rates of fire.

caliber have led to larger and heavier rounds which are more difficult for the "ammunition numbers" to handle.

The US Army's solution to this problem is the FAASV, which entered production in 1983, with introduction to service scheduled for 1985-86. The FAASV is based on the well-proven M109A2 chassis, but with a large armored housing in place of the turret. This housing contains removable vertical racks which are hoisted aboard by a 1,500lb (680kg) capacity, extendible-boom crane on the front of the vehicle. On arrival at the gun position, projectiles and charges are removed from these racks by an automatic stacker, assembled, fuzed, and then passed by an hydraulic conveyer directly into the supported gun.

The FAASV can carry 90 155mm projectiles and charges, or 48 8in rounds. The rate of passing rounds to the guns is 8 rounds per minute, which handsomely exceeds current rates of fire. An additional feature is that the armored rear door swings up to provide overhead protection during the transfer process.

More than 600 M992s are in service and production continues at a low rate. Ideally, the US Army would like to have one FAASV for each of its M109s, but budgetry constraints have so far prevented such a high level of procurement.

M9 ACE

Type: Armored Combat Earthmover (ACE).
Crew: One.
Dimensions: Length 20.5ft (6.24m); width 10.5ft (3.2m).
Weight: Empty 36,000lb (16,329kg); loaded 54,000lb (24,493kg).
Engine: Cummins V903 producing 295bhp.
Performance: Road speed 30mph (48km(h); amphibious 3mph (5km/h).

The ACE is a combat engineer tractor and is designed to enable combat formations to breach enemy earth obstacles, prepare fighting positions, create anti-tank ditches and keep supply routes open. Its armor allows it to carry out these tasks under fire and operate closely with tanks and mechanized infantry formations.

Bowen-McLaughlin-York delivered the first examples to the US Army in 1986, and the first full-production vehicles were handed over to major units in 1989. They performed well during the Gulf War, when they were

---

M985 HEMTT

Type: Heavy Expanded Mobility Tactical Truck (HEMTT).
Dimensions: Length 33.1ft (10.1m); width 7.87ft (2.4m).
Weight: Payload 10 tons (10,160kg).
Engine: Detroit Diesel V8 12-litre producing 445bhp.
Performance: Road speed 55 mph (88km/h); fording depth 4ft (1.21m).

To meet the requirement for a specialist vehicle to carry heavy palletized ammunition containers, such as MLRS rockets and Patriot missiles, the US Army developed the HEMTT family of vehicles. Its 8x8 drive also allows for resupply to take place as far forward as possible and gives US Army transportation units a signficant off-road capability. Some versions are fitted

Above: An M9 ACE on test. Note the armor protection for the driver.

used to break through the numerous Iraqi anti-tank ditches and sand berms built up in Kuwait and southern Iraq.

---

with cranes to speed the off-loading of pallets.

The Oshkosh Truck Company won its first HEMTT contract from the US Army in 1981, and a second was signed five years later. Some 11,000 have been delivered and production is planned to continue well into the mid-1990s Current production versions include the M985 MLRS resupply vehicle, M977 artillery ammunition carrier, M978 petrol tanker, M984E1 recovery vehicle and M938 Patriot missile support vehicle.

HEMTT's deployed to the Middle EAst during the Gulf War were regarded as the most capable in-theater logistic platform. Their superb cross-country performance led to them being referred to as "the ships of the desert".

Below: Unglamorous it may be, but the importance of the HEMITT family of support trucks to the modern-day, highly-mobile US Army ground forces cannot be overstressed.

Mines

The mine is a weapon which seems always to be on the verge of a major comeback, but never quite making it. There is no doubt as to its value in at least delaying (if not actually stopping) either armored or infantry advances or deployments. The major problem, however, is the time taken to lay mines, assuming that it is most unlikely that any will be

---

GEMSS
Ground-Emplaced Mine-Scattering System

All NATO armies have sought to enhance their ability to stop and defeat armored thrusts by the numerically superior Warsaw Pact forces. To this end, all forms of anti-tank weapons have been developed, and over the past decade there has been a marked revival of interest in anti-tank mines: interest both in the effect of the mines themselves and in rapid methods of laying them. The Ground-Emplaced Mine-Scattering System (GEMSS) is particularly effective, since it is mounted on a trailer that can be towed by any suitable tracked (M548 cargo carrier, M113 APC) or wheeled (5-ton truck) prime mover. GEMSS's primary purpose is quickly to lay minefields that will force attacking enemy armored vehicles to alter course into constricted areas where they will provide a rewarding target for killing weapons.

GEMSS is the M128 mine dispenser, holding up to 800 4lb (1.8kg) mines

mines, assuming that it is most unlikely that any will be laid in peacetime. Thus, great efforts have been devoted to rapid minelaying systems, using either mechanical layers or helicopters. Much attention is also being paid to delivering large quantities of very small mines ("minelets"), using artillery shells or missiles as the delivery agent.
The full range of US Army mines covers the spectrum from small anti-personnel mines, through anti-tank mines, to the Atomic Demolition Mines (ADMs) which will soon be withdrawn from Western Europe where they have been deployed for many years. The mine is an ideal defensive weapon—provided that it can be laid in time.

---

which are deployed at intervals of 32 or 64 yards (30 or 60m), the interval being determined by the rate of launch and the speed of the vehicle. The M128 dispenser is mounted on the M794 trailer.

The mines are laid on the surface and a 2,734 yard (2,500m) field can be laid in less than six hours. The anti-tank mine has a magnetic influence field; this means that it can attack the whole width of the target and does not need to be run over by the tracks. There is also an anti-personnel mine, a fragmentation weapon activated by automatically deployed trip-wire sensors. Both types of mine have anti-disturbance devices to inhibit clearance, but both also have a built-in self-destruct device which neutralizes the minefield after a pre-determined interval.

GEMSS will continue in frontline service for many years, although procurement has ceased.

Below: The Army's FASCAM (family of scatterable mines) program is designed to lay minefields rapidly to force enemy armor into "ambush" situations. It includes GEMSS (below) as well as mine systems seeded by artillery and aircraft.

General Logistics and Resupply

According to legend, a US Army general was being briefed on the then newly discovered "science" of logistics in the early 1940s. After listening for some time with increasing bewilderment he got to his feet and said to his staff: "I still don't know what these goddam logistics are—but, whatever they are, make sure I get a lot of them!" Any logistician would say that the attitudes of commanders and their operations staffs have changed little over the years: they still do not want to be bothered with the details, but heaven help the logistics specialist who fails to deliver the goods. The US Army's logistics problem is severe, because virtually any operation will be mounted at a very considerable distance from the Continental USA. Some of these can be carefully planned and prepared for in peace; eg, West Germany or South Korea, where in-place units are supported by a well-prepared logistic system. Other deployment options are recognized but are subject to peacetime limitations; for example, the Norwegians will not permit troops or stores to be positioned on their soil in peacetime. Finally, there are the open options, such as those facing the Rapid Deployment Force.

One of the logistic problems which causes US military planners most concern is the air/sea bridge across the North Atlantic, over which, in the early days of any future conflict or crisis, vast amounts of men and materiel would have to flow. The great increase in strength of the Soviet Navy is a direct threat to these plans, and, as in World War II, some of the most crucial battles will be fought in the open expanses of the Atlantic.

A second major logistic problem facing the US forces in Europe is that in peacetime the French will not permit US military stores to be landed in, or transported across, Metropolitan France. These stores must instead be

Above: A vehicle-mounted 25-ton crane on road test for the US Army. This is one of many thousands of support vehicles of differing types necessary to a modern army.

Left: M60 tanks are unloaded from a ship. US supply lines must use the vulnerable routes across the Pacific and Atlantic Oceans; this constitutes a major risk.

landed at North Sea ports and then moved by road and rail south to the US areas along a supply route which is parallel to—and dangerously near—the Inner German Border. This is a bad situation to be in, although it must be hoped that in war the French would relent. Further in-theater problems would arise in war with the roads being crammed with refugees and vehicles trying to move in the opposite direction to the military units and supplies.

One of the major logistic problems in terms of commodities is likely to be fuel. There has recently been a major switch-over to diesel to reduce demand—but there are vast numbers of vehicles and the allied logistic services are going to be very hard pressed to meet the demands. Obviously, reserves exist, but these would not sustain a war effort for very long. Thus, the fuel resupply lines back across the oceans to the point of production will be crucially important and, again, the Soviet Fleet seems poised to threaten all these.

A further problem for the logistic services in a future war will be that of dealing with casualties, especially those from chemical, biological, or nuclear attack. This is a task of awesome proportions.

Communications and Electronic Support

To ensure all the US Army's different combat units can operate successfully together on the battlefield, billions of dollars have been invested in sophisticated communications and computer equipment.

The scale of communications back-up available to the US Army can be gauged from the fact that at the start of the Operation *Desert Shield* deployment three USAF C-5 Galaxy transport plans were needed to airlift the documents describing US Central Command's communications plan (Joint Communications-Electronics Operating Instructions or Joint CEOI) to the Middle East. A similar complex plan for the 700 radio links needed to co-ordinate the invasion of Panama took a year to prepare.

Organizing communications links for even a division or brigade is now a complex business, involving hundreds of radio sets, frequencies, scrambling codes and code names. Divisions and corps have military intelligence units equipped with ground stations and aircraft, which are tasked with intercepting and jamming enemy radio transmissions. Considerable resources are also devoted to protecting friendly communications from enemy jamming and interception.

Increasingly, computers are being deployed to manage the mass of information available to commanders. A series of battle management systems are under development or in use by the US Army to co-ordinate different combat formations and weapons systems. The Forward Area Air Defence Command, Control and Intelligence (FAAD C²I) is designed to manage divisional air defence weapons. To look after logistics there is the Combat Service Support Control System (CSSCS). The Advanced Field Artillery Tactical Data System (AFATDS) will allow commanders to quickly lay down fire and manage the supply of ammunition to their guns. For real-time monitoring of intelligence from spotter posts, airborne radar and other sources, the All Source Analysis System (ASAS) is under development. To bring these diverse systems together there is the Army Tactical Command and Control

Below: The sheer compactness of today's lap-top computers has proved to be a great boost for US Army units operating in the field, as was evident during Operation *Desert Storm*.

Above: In the vast, often featureless deserts of Saudi Arabia, Iraq and Kuwait, reliable communications systems such as this Single Channel Ground and Airborne Radio System were vital.

System (ATCCS), which gives high level commanders a clearer picture of the overall battle as it develops.

To interlink these systems, high-capacity satellite, cable and radio links have been developed. While battlefield facsimile machines and other modern communications have undoubtedly transformed the ability of commanders to respond to rapidly changing events, many officers recognize the danger of "information overload" paralysing the command process.

One area where computer technology has had a dramatic effect is counter-battery fire. The Firefinder AN/TPQ-36 and AN/TPQ-37 locating radars were linked up by the Army Data Distribution System to put devastating MLRS fire down on Iraqi artillery batteries within seconds of them opening fire. ▶

Above: The ability of a forward fire team to transmit/receive target data is an absolute prerequisite in modern warfare. In this instance, information on enemy force levels is being fed back to headquarters by a BGM-71 TOW team for analysis.

Right: As with the miniaturization of computers, so satellite communications have become more available to frontline forces thanks to man-portable units. Illustrated is one such unit, complete with carrying case, being readied for transmission by *Delta Force* troops in Saudi Arabia.

▶   The US Army's Military Satellite Communications program provides high-level commanders with secure strategic communications anywhere in the world. Terminals are becoming smaller and most are now portable on trucks or in tactical transport aircraft. Man-portable rapid burst satellite transmission systems are used by Special Operations Forces behind enemy lines to protect them from direction-finding equipment.

Space technology was put into practical use by almost every US soldier taking part in Operation *Desert Storm* thanks to the NAVSTAR Global Positioning System (GPS). Most US vehicles, aircraft, ships and many infantry squads were equipped with GPS terminals to allow the operator to instantaneously read off their location from its LED display. This (almost) infallible system transformed navigation in the desert and allowed units to move with great confidence at night. "If it could make coffee, I'd marry it" said one US Army sergeant.

More than 8,000 such commercially produced receiver terminals (called "sluggers" by ordinary soldiers) were purchased by the Pentagon during Operation *Desert Shield* to allow as many units as possible to benefit from GPS. Unfortunately this meant the navigation data transmitted by the satellite could not be encrypted to prevent the Iraqis using the system as well. This, however, was considered an acceptable trade-off by US commanders in the field.

The reliability of GPS became legendary during *Desert Storm* and it was responsible for the high accuracy of US artillery units, which were able to calaculate fire missions with great precision. The MLRS, for example, has a GPS terminal built into its fire control system to allow its crews to navigate and plot their fire. The crews of older artillery pieces had to rely on the hand-held terminals to make use of GPS.

Uniforms and Personal Equipment

The US Army prides itself on providing its soldiers with the best uniforms and personal equipment money can buy, to enable them to fight effectively and survive under all battle conditions, anywhere in the world.

In the early-1990s, over 43 research and development projects for new clothing and individual equipment were approved by the US Army Chief of Staff, including laser eye protection, ballistic vests, aircrew cold weather uniforms and air drop containers. Research is also constantly carried out on improving equipment that is already in service, such as the hot weather battle dress uniforms (BDU), combat boot sock and the wet weather parka/trousers. The diversity of the items being developed gives some idea of the scope and scale of the US Army's efforts in this vital field. During the Fiscal Year 1991, nine new items were accepted into service, including the 40mm grenade vest, sleeping bag pad, parachutists rough

terrain suit, intermediate cold/wet boots and an intermediate cold/wet glove.

The most famous uniform items to enter service in recent years are the desert BDUs. They were first fielded in 1982 but attracted considerable attention during the Gulf War. The Defence Personal Support Center, Philadelphia, developed a replacement for the original desert BDUs because they were considered too bright for use in the Saudi Arabian desert. The original six-coloured BDU is replaced by a new three-colour uniform that does not stand out against the natural background. A new Type II desert boot which is lighter and keeps the sand out better is also being introduced. The rapid deployment of half a million US servicemen to the Middle East during the Gulf crisis put a great strain on the supply of desert uniforms and equipment and many troops who deployed to Saudi Arabia from Germany never received desert BDUs or desert boots until after the ceasefire. Some troops complained that there was not much point issuing desert uniforms ▶

Below: Images of US Army soldiers wearing the latest tricolor version of the desert battle dress uniform were transmitted around the world in 1990-91, as Operation *Desert Sheild* and *Desert Storm* were initiated to rid Kuwait of Iraqi forces.

▶ because the US Army was still using green-coloured personal tool-bearing equipment and gas mask carriers, which made the wearer stand out against the light desert.

For many years the US Army has lead the world in the development of training systems based on laser technology. The Multiple Integrated Laser Engagement System (MILES) allows highly realistic training to be carried out by all types of combat units, from infantry squads up to divisions. Infantry, combat vehicles and aircraft are fitted with eye-safe low power lasers which simulate their weapons' characteristics. Individual soldiers and vehicles are fitted with detectors that trigger alarms or smoke bombs to simulate hits. MILES provides realistic evidence during exercises that hits have been achieved and gives a real incentive for troops to stay under cover.

The Gulf crisis, however, pin-pointed many weaknesses in the US Army's protection against nuclear, biological and chemical (NBC) warfare. Much NBC

Above: A uniform that no soldier in the US Army wants to have to wear — but one which could save his or her life. Covered from head to toe in the standard-issue NBC suit and hood, and with their individual M17 respirators plugged in, a trio of servicemen protect themselves against the perils of an NBC attack.

equipment was found to be out-of-date or to have passed its shelf life. Many US troops resorted to buying caged canaries because of a lack of confidence in their old NBC detection and warning systems. A series of crash programs were instituted to rectify the situation, including buying off-the-shelf items from Britain, such as Chemical Agent Monitors (CAM). The US Army's NBC suit and M17 respirator with hood was also identified as being inferior to the British suit which has an integral hood. To change respirator canisters on the M17 the wearer has to remove the hood and ►

▶ thus increase the risk of exposure to chemical agents, but the new M40 mask has an external canister. A new mask is also being fitted to allow Apache helicopter crews to use the AH-64A's integrated vision systems while wearing a respirator.

A wide range of remote chemical detectors and alarms, chemical decontamination kits, radiation monitors and NBC-proof shelters for hospitals and headquarters are currently in service or under development by industry and the US Army's Chemical Research, Development and Engineering Center, at the Aberdeen Proving Grounds, Maryland.

With more and more Third World countries developing chemical weapons, or the "poor man's nuclear bomb" as they are euphemistically known, the US Army recognizes the increasing importance of providing effective defense against these deadly weapons.

Right: The sheer diversity of operating climates experienced by US Army personnel is reflected in this view of troops in full cold-weather dress, including snow shoes.

Below: The US Army has fully embraced the use of MILES as a training aid. Note the laser unit on this M60's muzzle.

▶ Web equipment has evolved gradually over the years, but even the Americans have not yet found a really satisfactory answer to the problem of providing a really comfortable method of carrying the impedimenta needed by a modern soldier. As was discovered by British infantrymen during the 1982 war in the Falklands, an APC or truck will not always be available to carry it all.

Much publicity is given to the overpressure systems now being fitted to all AFVs to ensure a degree of NBC protection for the crew. The vast majority of soldiers on the modern battlefield will, however, not have such protection, and will still have to rely on respirators and protective suits. In the early 1980s, the US Army found itself so lacking in this area that it had to buy some 200,000 British Mark 3 NBC suits and boots for US troops in Western Europe, to cover the gap pending issue of new American equipment. What still has to be determined—and not just by the US Army—is just how long soldiers will be able to continue fighting and working in such conditions, because nobody can pretend that wearing the full NBC equipment for protracted periods is anything other than a very trying experience.

Most US Army uniforms and items of personal equipment are well-designed and popular with the troops. There has been a noticeable increase in the smartness and bearing of American soldiers since the bad days of the aftermath of Vietnam, and they now—especially since the success in Grenada—appear proud and confident once again, which bodes well for their many allies around the world.

Below: US Army infantrymen on exercise in northern Norway move equipment on a Norwegian "pulk". This is just one of the very many deployment options for which the Army is constantly training.

Above: An infantry soldier in his combat suit and boots, holding an M16 rifle. The helmet is the new model, made of Kevlar, which is lighter, more comfortable, and offers better protection.

OTHER SUPER-VALUE MILITARY GUIDES IN THIS SERIES

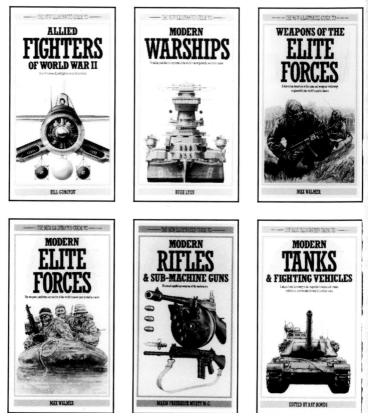